BURSTING
with
Joy

Discovering Universal
Truths Through Our Special Son

By Joan Broggi

Ferne Press

Bursting with Joy:
Discovering Universal Truths Through Our Special Son
Copyright © 2010 by Joan Broggi
Printed in Canada
Layout and cover design by Kimberly Franzen

Summary: A mother recounts the parental struggles and emotions involved in raising a special needs child, as well as the life lessons her son taught her family along the way.

Library of Congress Cataloging-in-Publication Data
Broggi, Joan
Bursting with Joy: Discovering Universal Truths Through Our Special Son/Joan Broggi – First Edition
ISBN-13: 978-1-933916-53-8
ISBN-10: 1-933916-53-8
1. Family and Relationships 2. Epilepsy 3. Positive Thinking
4. Special Education 5. Inspirational 6. Biography
I. Broggi, Joan II. Bursting with Joy: Discovering Universal Truths Through Our Special Son
Library of Congress Control Number: 2010920383

Some of the chapter headings in this book were originally published in a slightly different form in *On Death and Dying*, Dr. Elisabeth Kübler-Ross (New York: Macmillan, 1969).

FERNE PRESS

Ferne Press is an imprint of Nelson Publishing & Marketing
366 Welch Road, Northville, MI 48167
www.nelsonpublishingandmarketing.com
(248) 735-0418

Dedicated to our son, Alex,
who taught us that with
love and compassion,
we can move out of
despair and fear,
and into hope.

Contents

*"We enjoy the warmth because we have
been cold. We appreciate light because we
have been in darkness. By the same token,
we can experience joy because we have known sorrow."*

David Weatherford

Author's Note

Alex's high school senior picture.

This story encompasses the first nineteen years of my son's life. Although Alex was born healthy, his life journey took a different path than the one I had envisioned for him. Looking at his high school senior pictures, you would probably find him to be a good-looking, tall young man with a bright future ahead of him. You are correct on all accounts, but if you were to meet him or hold a conversation with him, you would notice many things different from typical boys his age. He has an extremely limited vocabulary, he is unable to understand much of what you say to him, and he has an awkward gait when he walks.

Alex's mental age is about the same as that of an eight-year-old. He has been enrolled in special education for most of his life.

I could tell you all the things he will never be able to do, but I would rather focus on all the things he *can* do. He has taught us more in his nineteen years of life than we ever could have taught him.

The first five sections of this book correspond to the stages of grief humans experience as we go through life-changing or traumatic events. As outlined by Dr. Elisabeth Kübler-Ross in her 1969 book *On Death and Dying*, these stages are Denial, Anger, Bargaining, Depression, and Acceptance. I've added a sixth stage: Joy. By the end of this book, you will understand why.

It is with sincere gratitude that the author wishes to thank you, the reader of this book, for taking the time to read our story. My desire is to create a deeper appreciation and respect for people with disabilities and to change public perception. They are *not* a burden on society, but if given the opportunity, have something to offer all of us.

Denial. . .

The stage of grief where you exhibit disbelief.

"This isn't really happening to me, is it?"

1
The Birthday Present

"Can we get Daddy an ice cream cake today like you promised, Mommy?" Kellie asked.

"And some boons," piped in Nicholas.

"They are called ba-lloons," Kellie corrected him.

On August 30, 1990, I woke up to my two preschoolers looking for breakfast. Kellie was three and a half years old, with a beautiful smile and a head full of blonde curls. Nicholas was not quite two yet and was an all rough-and-tumble boy. They were excited because it was Daddy's birthday today, and although he was already at work for the day, they knew we would celebrate when he got home for dinner.

I personally did not want to get out of bed. I was exhausted after an uncomfortable night of tossing and turning, and sweat poured over my body. I was eight and a half months pregnant with our third child. I still had two weeks to go before my due date, and I wanted to make my husband Nick's birthday special! But it was late August, it was hot, and I realized I was soaking wet...and so was my bed.

"Oh my goodness," I said to the kids, "I think I just peed the bed."

They started to giggle. "Mommies don't pee in bed," Kellie told Nicholas.

"You're right," I said, "I think my water broke."

After consulting with my mother and the doctors, I realized I had to get to the hospital. "But what about Daddy's birthday?" Kellie wanted to know. "We have to go get his present!"

"We'll get it later," I promised her, and off we went.

Seven hours, many walks through the hospital hallways to get labor going, two warm baths, and some Pitocin later, Alex Anthony was born. As soon as I delivered him, the doctor asked my husband if he would like to cut the cord. Of course, he obliged. And then I heard the most wonderful noise a mother could hear, the sweet cry of my newborn baby who just entered the world. Caught up in the moment, I hadn't even realized yet if I had given birth to a boy or a girl.

"Well, what did I have?"

In unison, the doctor, nurses, and my husband said, "It's a boy." I smiled and let out a sigh of relief, for I was glad the labor pains had subsided and my baby had finally arrived.

The baby was cleaned up and then placed on my chest. I remember looking down at this most beautiful, blonde, blue-eyed, healthy newborn baby boy and falling in love. For me, the maternal bond of a mother holding her newborn infant for the very first time was instant. And once again, for the third time now, I was experiencing one of the most joyous events in my life.

I was holding my newborn son and grinning from ear to ear as my husband walked over. He bent down, kissed me, and then kissed Alex on the forehead and smiled.

I looked at him and said, "Honey, I'm sorry we didn't get to celebrate your birthday today with dinner and a cake like I had originally planned, but I did get you the best present I could possibly think of to give you," and I handed him our precious little boy.

"Are you kidding me?" he replied. "This is the absolute best birthday present ever!"

I got choked up at his remarks and our eyes welled up as he cradled Alex in his arms. We had always talked about wanting a big family and our family was surely growing now with the birth of our third child.

We had the same hopes and dreams for him as we had for our other children, and we surely knew that he would bring so much joy and pleasure into our lives like our other children already had.

Alex was precious, to be sure, and we were extremely grateful. My husband handed him back to me and as I gazed at him, so peaceful and calm, lying in my arms as content as can be, I was euphoric. What a remarkable gift my husband and I had just received—and on Nick's thirtieth birthday. How perfect was that?

Little did I realize what was to come or how this child would turn our lives upside down. And yet, in the process, how he would also surpass any hopes, dreams, and expectations I could have ever had for him, and in ways I never imagined possible!

2

The First Seizure

Six months had passed and Alex had an appointment with his pediatrician. He was due for his immunizations and I wasn't looking forward to the visit. As a mom, I had always wished I could take the shots for my children. I knew it wouldn't hurt me nearly as much as it hurt them. But I knew this couldn't be. He got his DPT (diphtheria, pertussis, and tetanus) shot that day and home we went. We were told it was possible he may run a fever as a result of the shots and we were prepared for that (or so we thought).

A few days later my husband and I were going to bed around ten o'clock. All the kids had been sleeping for a few hours by now and as I looked over to Alex's cradle in the corner of our room, I noticed it was shaking back and forth. As I got closer, I heard a humming noise coming from my baby.

"Oh my goodness! What's wrong with Alex?" I yelled to Nick who was washing up in the bathroom. Nick came running. He looked in the crib and saw Alex's tiny body jerking and shaking.

We immediately called 911 and I went into the ambulance with him, not realizing at that time that this would be the first of many trips to the ER. The seizure stopped en route and I looked at my innocent, fragile baby with an oxygen mask covering his tiny face. I felt so very afraid and helpless all at the same time. My precious baby's perfect, pink complexion had turned a shade of blue and that completely terrified me. I could not take my eyes off of him. I was fixated, just staring and praying and praying some more. My body was numb. I just wanted to cradle my baby in my arms at that very moment and tell him it was going to be okay and that I loved him so very much and I would do everything in my power to prevent this from ever happening to him again. But I couldn't hold him and that alone hurt immensely. He just lay there, very lethargic and still, breathing the oxygen in and out of his tiny body.

"Are you okay?" the ER tech asked me. I continued to stare, in a state of shock I suppose, at my son, not really knowing what to think at that point. I didn't answer, but just sort of nodded my head.

Am I okay? I thought. *I can't believe you even asked me that! I wanted to scream, No I am NOT okay! This is not good and I wish it would have never happened! I just want my baby to be okay and then...yeah...maybe, just maybe...I will be okay.*

It was much later on that my husband did admit to me how very worried he was that Alex wouldn't be okay. He actually thought there was a chance Alex might not make it. I'm so glad he did not tell me that in the days and weeks that followed because those thoughts never even entered my mind at that time. I never allowed myself to go there. My husband and I are different in that respect. He says I live in the moment and deal with things as they come. This much is true, for I feel we cannot change the inevitable, but we can change how we react to it.

> **Attitude is important and I was trying to keep a positive one, hoping for the best possible outcome.**

Nick, on the other hand, is always looking at the big picture, and thinking of the future outcome of any given situation and how the problems at hand will impact it. He considers every possible scenario, good or bad, perhaps so he will be better equipped to deal with the end result.

As we entered the ER at the hospital and Alex was wheeled in, his tiny body on that massive stretcher, I was as close by his side as I could possibly be. I couldn't let my eyes leave his, not even for a moment. He was sleeping now and breathing a little heavier than normal as they placed him in a room. I was extremely worried. The doctor entered within minutes of our arrival and so did my husband. I was glad about that, but at the same time so very nervous and hoping for some answers.

"It's a febrile seizure," the ER doctor told us. They did a spinal tap, monitored him for awhile, and gave us a prescription for Phenobarbital after giving Alex a dose. We were told that Phenobarbital is an anti-epileptic drug used to control seizures. "Follow up with your pediatrician in a few days and we'll wean the Phenobarb from there," they said.

Phenobarb, febrile seizure, epilepsy. These words were all Greek to me. *What had just happened to my son? Why? And worst of all, was it going to happen again?* These thoughts kept running through my head. I couldn't believe this was even happening! And, worst of all, I wasn't really getting the answers that I was hoping for.

3
How Can We "Fix" Him?

Four years later, Alex has had many more seizures since the initial one. Actually, too many to count. He had seizures when he was tired, or when he overexerted himself, or was running a fever. Or for just no reason at all. We were always trying to figure out the when and why of it all, but we never could. I documented every single one, in binder after binder, and recorded how long they lasted and where he was when they happened. I rarely let him out of my sight and became an overbearing, overprotective mom. He couldn't run off to play like his older siblings without being constantly watched and monitored. It got overwhelming for all of us.

We took him to the pediatrician way too often. Because of his weak immune system, he always got sick—flu, colds, and pneumonia, to name a few. And with each illness came the seizures. He would spike a fever and go into a tonic-clonic seizure. These are also known as grand mal seizures and are the most severe type. In the tonic phase, Alex would cry out and collapse to the ground. The clonic phase consisted of repeated jerking of the limbs, body, and head. The postictal phase is the period immediately following the seizure, when Alex would become fatigued and limp. He would sleep for many hours afterward. During tonic-clonic seizures, there is also a loss of consciousness and the possibility of loss of bladder control—each of which happened all too often for Alex.

This became a constant in Alex's life and ours. Sometimes if he was sick, he would have as many as six or seven grand mal seizures in a day and other times he would have as few as three or four in a week. But they always came, were often random, and came without warning. They affected everything about him mentally. Whether he had one or more seizures, with each one came the setbacks. The progress he had been making seemed to become lost and we would have to reteach him many things, such as the alphabet and counting. As if it wasn't bad enough that he was even having the seizures, and way too frequently, now we had to deal with the loss of some of his acquired cognitive functioning in the process.

We spent countless hours in the ER—he fell and cracked his head open twice, requiring many stitches to close the open wound on the side of his head, which to this day remains scarred.

We took him to countless doctors and neurologists looking for answers and trying to "fix" our son, but to no avail.

We tried countless drugs to "control" the seizures but could never stop them completely. We tried the ketogenic diet, a strict diet that is high in fat and low in protein and carbohydrates. The body goes into a process called ketosis, which is when the body breaks down fats instead of carbohydrates to use for energy. Although researchers are unsure how exactly ketosis inhibits seizures, the diet has been remarkably successful for some people with epilepsy. But not for Alex! He stayed on the diet for almost two years and although we did see some decrease in his seizure activity, it wasn't enough to keep him on it and warrant such a drastic lifestyle change for him and our entire family. It wasn't easy...ever. Dealing with the seizures was overwhelming and consumed our lives.

We were told simply that he had epilepsy.

What is epilepsy? I didn't even know!

I soon learned that epilepsy is diagnosed when a person has

two or more unprovoked seizures. It's a disorder of the brain, and although some cases can be linked to an identifiable cause, most cases cannot. This was our scenario.

4
Kindergarten

It was the fall of 1995. My husband had recently accepted a new job and we had relocated from Michigan, where all of our family lived, to the Princeton, New Jersey area. We had only been living there about five months and had spent most of the summer exploring this new area of the East Coast. We also had a new addition to our family—a baby girl named Angela, who was not quite one year old. We would travel to the Jersey Shore on the weekends to build sandcastles and collect seashells; this became one of Alex's favorite activities. We would also travel into New York City to see Broadway plays or to explore a museum with the kids. We were embracing our move away from loved ones and enjoying the time we spent together as a family.

Alex was five years old now and although he was still having a couple of seizures a week, they weren't as frequent as what we had previously experienced. Under a neurologist's care we seemed to have found a good mix of antiseizure drugs for him. His milestones, when he wasn't seizing that is, for the most part weren't that different than my other children's at that age. He knew the alphabet, could count quite well, and enjoyed being read to, but could not read by himself quite yet.

It was now time to enroll the kids in school for the upcoming year. Kellie was eight years old and would be entering the third grade.

Nicholas was six and would be going into first grade, and Alex had just turned five and was ready for kindergarten (or so we thought!).

Alex's first day of kindergarten.

A few months into the school year, things seemed to be going smoothly. Alex's seizures were not as frequent and he seemed happy to be in school. One morning I was feeding Angela breakfast when I got a phone call from Mrs. Aaron, Alex's kindergarten teacher.

"We need to talk," she spoke into the phone.

"Okay," I said, "when would you like to meet?"

"As soon as possible," she said. At that moment, I wondered what was going on and knew at the same time that whatever it was wasn't good.

Some time later, as I was driving over to the school to meet with his teacher, I had a million thoughts racing through my mind. Although I knew, deep in my heart, that the constant seizing that Alex had experienced over the last few years did have a profound impact on his mental capacity, I did not want to think about it and often pushed it from my mind. I saw this happening with the passing of each seizure bringing him down both mentally and physically as well.

> **As his mother, I did not want to admit that he was capable of anything less than the milestones he should be achieving for his age.**

As I greeted his teacher and sat down to discuss Alex's situation, I was put off immediately by her attitude. Her demeanor was not one I was expecting. She was quite direct with me from the get-go that Alex did not belong in her kindergarten classroom. This caught me a bit off guard. As a young mother I just wanted all of my children to go through the normal stages of life that all children experience, like attending kindergarten when they turn five. At the time, it seemed she didn't care about how I felt. She just got to the point. I don't know if I can even recall everything she said to me that day. I remember phrases like "he doesn't interact with the other children" and "he can't really follow two- and three-step directions," and words kept spinning through my head like "early intervention" and "other programs that would better suit his needs."

What was she saying to me and why couldn't my son remain in a normal kindergarten class like his peers?

When I left the meeting with her, I did not walk away comforted and assured, knowing I could go back to her with further questions and concerns. I came away frustrated and upset. I knew I had a lot to wrap my head around, for I really had no idea what early intervention and special education were all about. All I knew was that I did not want my child placed in that category.

Did she want him removed from her classroom for his sake or hers? I had to wonder. *Why didn't she show me a little more encouragement and empathy?* At the time, that was what I needed.

> **Looking back, I now realize she did have his best interests in mind, and as an educator she was only trying to find the best placement for him.**

I only wish she would have treated me with a gentler approach. Yes, I was in denial of my son's diagnosis. Little did I know at the time, but things were going to get much worse before they got better.

5

The Life-Changing Event

Winter of 1996 was a cold and snowy one, which wasn't anything new to us transplanted Michiganders, but it was to our Jersey neighbors. They weren't used to all the snow, especially when it came all at once as it did one particular weekend in January. It started on a Saturday night and snowed and snowed and snowed until Monday night. When all was said and done, I think we had accumulated twenty-four to thirty-six inches of snow on the ground. You couldn't even see our mailbox at the end of the driveway. It was the most snow I had ever seen in my lifetime, but as awesome and beautiful as it was, it was also annoying because it had to be shoveled. And my husband was heading out of town.

Happy, I was not! Stuck in the house, sole adult, snowbound, with four young children and a driveway full of massive amounts of snow that needed to be shoveled! Not a pretty picture for a young mom. My kids, however, were loving it.

"Can we build a snowman?" Kellie kept asking.

"I want to build a snow tunnel," Nicholas piped in.

"Okay, get your snow gear on," I told my eight- and six-year-olds.

Alex went into the laundry room with his sister and brother to get his winter clothes on. "Hey, buddy," I said to him, "Don't you want to watch Barney?"

"Nope, I play in the snow," he said matter-of-factly.

"But Mom," Kellie piped in, "should he?" She was wise for all of her eight years and knew what the outcome of him joining us could be; it happened way too many times before and we had to be very cautious of overheating and overexerting Alex. These were triggers of seizures for him.

"Maybe just for a few minutes," I told Kellie and Nicholas. "You two start the snowman and Alex can come out and put on the carrot for his nose." That was to be our plan, anyway. Angela was down for a nap and we'd be right outside the front door. Harmless, I thought at the time.

Because Nick was out of town, the neighbors came over to help clear the snow from our driveway. It was very kind of them and I was grateful. The two older kids were playing with some neighbor friends and rolling the snowballs for "Frosty" when they rang the doorbell.

"Alex can come out with the carrot now," Nicholas said.

I bundled Alex up, but not too much, and got ready myself. "We can't stay out too long, because the baby will be up soon" was the excuse I gave Alex to get him back inside soon. It worked too, because he was okay with it. We went into the front yard and he was so excited to join his siblings in the mounds of snow. It was quite enjoyable to watch them, but I was nervous. Alex did fine for about twenty minutes, and then down he went, limp as a rag, into the snow. The seizure wasn't quite full-blown yet and I carried him inside the front door and began to peel his layers of clothes off. Then, BAM, he went into a grand mal seizure. This wasn't uncommon, but after the first one, he went into another. "Go get Mrs. B!" I screamed to Kellie to get our neighbor. "I'll call 911." Although the weather was bad, surprisingly the EMS truck made it quite quickly. Unfortunately, Alex could not stop seizing! He'd stop one seizure and within minutes would go into another, with each one lasting three to five minutes...which seemed like hours at the time.

"We need to transport," was all I could hear as I worried about my son. The neighbors came over to help with the other kids. Not even thinking about how I would get home, I went into the ambulance with Alex. Usually I would follow in my car once he was stabilized, but not this time. He was still seizing, and this seizure lasted more than thirty minutes. It was the most dreadful thing I'd ever experienced. I felt so very helpless. And I didn't know what was going to become of my son—my blue-eyed, blonde, beautiful five-year-old baby boy!

They injected him with a drug called Diastat to finally stop the seizures. The neurologist told me he went into status epilepticus.

"What's that?" I demanded to know.

The neurologist explained to me that status epilepticus is a life-threatening condition in which seizures do not stop after thirty minutes or the patient goes immediately into one seizure after another and doesn't regain consciousness in between.

"These prolonged seizures can injure the brain as well as cause heart, lung, and kidney problems," he told me.

That's what was happening to my child? I couldn't believe it. *What was the damage he suffered as a result of all these seizures?* I didn't want to believe this was actually happening. I did not want things to be the way they were, but I needed to face the facts and get a grip on the reality of the situation.

They finally got the seizures to stop and Alex went to sleep and was very groggy. He was admitted to the hospital and stayed for many days. He was given drugs to stop the seizures and the drugs he was currently on were increased. He was hooked up to all these wires on his head with a bandage around them to monitor future seizure activity, and he slept a lot. I, unfortunately, did not sleep a lot. I prayed and never left his side.

My mother came to town on the next flight out of Detroit and stayed with my three other children. She was wonderful! Nick returned early from his business trip and met me at the hospital, more worried than I (as if that was even possible). I remembered the night he walked into Alex's hospital room. I had crawled up into Alex's bed to lie with him because I just wanted to hug him and keep him safe. Nick walked over to the bed and kissed each of us on the forehead. Alex didn't budge, for he was sound asleep (the drugs made him very lethargic). But I jumped up.

"It's okay, it's me," Nick said.

I grabbed him and hugged him like there was no tomorrow and sobbed quietly into his chest for what seemed like hours.

"I'm going to take you home to get some rest," he told me, but I was insisting that I didn't want to leave Alex. "I'll be with him, it'll be okay. You need to go home to rest and be with your mom and the kids," he asserted. He was right, and I went home quite reluctantly.

The next several days were a blur as we watched Alex get EEGs and brain scans and new medication and blood drawn and finger pricks. They were trying to find the right mix of antiseizure drugs to keep all the seizing at bay. It was truly a process of trial and error, I believe on the doctor's part, to see what would work and what would not. Through it all, Alex was quite resilient. He handled all the procedures and testing he had to endure better than I could have ever expected. He was very brave when they drew his blood and this truly amazed me.

Why isn't he screaming and crying and ranting and raving? I couldn't help but wonder. That did surprise me, at first. But then he was always such a calm, peaceful, happy child that I shouldn't have doubted him.

> **When they are small, we show our children the world through our eyes, but I was realizing now that he was showing me the world through his.**

His attitude at the tender age of five and a half had already far surpassed mine. Through it all he was quite a trooper. It was hard to swallow what he went through. I wouldn't wish that on anybody!

Alex was released after about a week, and thank goodness the seizures had stopped. "He's been through a lot, he's on a lot of drugs, and he needs to rest" was what we were told when we finally got the go-ahead to take him home. I was so happy to be out of there and to go home and be a family again, not knowing how different things would become.

But things were going to change now, and not for the better. From here on out, Alex would never be quite the same. As a result of all the clusters of seizures he experienced in such a short time, he had suffered some brain damage. He now seemed to be taking five steps backward for every single step forward. Any milestones he reached before, such as saying his ABCs and counting to twenty, had to be relearned. And this time it wasn't an easy process. He seemed to have lost so much more, cognitively, than he ever had before.

The next several years were tough, but we managed to move forward. We enrolled him in a brand-new, state-of-the-art school for children with special needs. We learned more about early intervention and IEPs (individualized education plans) and epilepsy and seizure drugs. This was a whole new world to us, and one we weren't prepared to embrace. We had three other perfectly healthy, beautiful, intelligent children and now we had to deal with one that was still beautiful, but healthy and intelligent no longer applied.

Anger . . .

The stage of grief where you feel let down,
mad, and frustrated.

**"I do not
like what is
happening."**

6

The Darkest Day

After we truly realized that Alex had suffered some brain damage, it took some time for us to get over the anger that consumed us—anger over what had happened to cause him to lose some of his cognitive functioning, and anger toward the reality that he may never regain what he lost or advance much further in his cognitive skills.

Actually, I was beyond anger and I did not like what was happening to him, and to me for that matter! There was this fear of the unknown. *Will he get better once we get over this latest hurdle? Or will he get worse?*

Alex was still heavily drugged to keep the seizures at bay and wasn't my fun-loving, happy child anymore. That hurt me more than anything. We kept him home from school for weeks now until he returned, at least somewhat, to his former self.

One afternoon, my oldest brother called. We were still living in New Jersey, away from family, and although it was nice to hear from them, it was hard not having that family support nearby, especially on the difficult days. After giving him an update of Alex's dire condition and the fact that we could have lost him, I vented to him about how difficult the last few weeks had been.

"Would your life be easier without him?" my brother spoke into the phone.

"How could you *even* ask me that?" I raised my voice back at him.

My brother was good at that. Asking you a thought-provoking question to get you to think deeper, come to grips with your reality, and hopefully, in the end, come up with some sort of solution. I knew that was what he was doing here. But, still, it angered me and he could tell. He was not even a parent himself and from the outside looking in I was sure he thought our lives would be less pain-filled and much easier to handle if we didn't have Alex and all his health problems to deal with. This phone call was definitely striking a nerve with me. He was trying to be supportive and understanding and I knew that. But he was asking me to contemplate things I would rather not. So after much thought I told him the following:

"As a mother, I could never imagine my life without any of my children. Losing Alex would cut a hole so deep into my heart and leave such a huge void in my life that could never be filled. Same goes for any of my children.

> **Although Alex's illness has put me through some pretty dark days, I could never imagine him not being a part of my life or me being a part of his.**

So to answer your question—no, my life would not be easier without him."

"Well," he said, "then I guess what you need to do now is to get past the anger that is currently eating away at you before it totally consumes you."

"What do you mean?" I demanded to know, but at the same time I knew how right he was. I was only hurting myself by being so very angry at what was happening and that wasn't doing Alex, or any of us for that matter, any good.

"It's okay to get mad or frustrated," he said, "but at some point you have to get past it and move on."

We finished our conversation. I thanked him for calling and

hung up the phone. I ran upstairs to my bedroom, jumped onto my king-sized bed, and proceeded to punch my pillow.

I hated that this was my situation.

I hated the way I felt.

I hated what my brother was saying to me.

I was having a major fight with reality and I needed a larger pillow to muffle my screams.

I guess my brother is right, I thought to myself as I lay on my bed. I can't let this anger get the best of me, for it surely was doing just that. I knew I had to somehow channel all my negative energy into something more productive. There were setbacks, to be sure, and I felt defeated. But I had to get past that for all of my children. The fact that Alex could go from an innocent, "normal" child with a bright future ahead of him to one that was struggling to survive was heartbreaking to think about.

> **In order for things to change, I had to choose to get past the anger and frustration that had its hold on me.**

It was after this incident that I decided not to make a bad situation worse. *What good would that do?* My anger was slowly beginning to subside. Although all four of my children make my life worth living, I finally realized I had to love each one of them for who they are, not what I wanted them to be.

Even on Alex's darkest days, my mom always said to me, "This too shall pass." Raising him has not been easy and I'm the first to admit this. But, I gave him life and I wouldn't trade my time with him for anything in the world. On his good days he brings so much sunshine into our lives, and I admit that on the bad, tough, seizure-filled days, we see the rain. But again, as my mother used to tell us when we were kids, "You never see the rainbow without the rain." I'm a firm believer that people come into our lives for a reason and although I don't know what the future holds for him, I know my life has changed because of him.

It was becoming clear to me that I needed to always be there for my son and help him overcome any obstacles that came his way. He deserved nothing less, and as his mother I was going to provide that for him.

7

The Monster

"You've created a monster!" my father-in-law screamed at me as he slammed his hand on the kitchen table.

"Don't talk about my son like that!" I screamed back as I tried to come between him and Alex. I was so very angry at that moment—angry at the scene that had just transpired and at the fact that all of this even had to happen in the first place. Worst of all was that this wasn't the first time it had happened, and surely, I knew, it wouldn't be the last.

Moments earlier, Alex was eating dinner at the kitchen table and the TV was on in the adjacent family room for him to view as he ate. My father-in-law, who was staying with us at the time, reached for the TV remote control that was sitting on the corner of the table to change the channel to the news. At the time, Alex was engrossed in an episode of *SpongeBob Squarepants* as he finished his dinner. As his grandfather reached for the remote, Alex grabbed it before he could get it, nipping his hand in the process.

"Don't you ever hit me!" My father-in-law screamed at his grandson. "You need to go to your room, *now!*" he yelled even louder. Hearing the commotion going on in the kitchen, Nick entered the picture. As my father-in-law continued screaming at Alex to go to his room and give him the remote, Nick interjected, "Leave him alone!" That's when he told us that we had created a monster.

After some heated words exchanged between Nick and his father, I got Alex to give me the remote and took his dessert away from him. This made him quite mad and also did not satisfy his grandfather, for he wanted the consequences to be more severe. I also explained to Alex that he needed to apologize to his grandfather for taking the remote from him. He sat at the kitchen table and sulked because he no longer had the TV channel on that he wanted and his ice cream dessert was taken away. But he got the message.

In the meantime, my father-in-law retreated to the corner chair of the family room to sulk, because evidently he didn't get his way either.

> It was definitely necessary to teach Alex a lesson, but Nick and I felt it had to be kept simple enough for him to understand.

My father-in-law did not understand this. I know that he cares about his grandson, but I also realize it is very difficult for him to accept Alex's limitations. When he looks at Alex he expects him to act his age for he wants him to be "normal" like his other grandchildren.

That same night I was putting Alex to bed. After I tucked him in and we said his prayers, I told him goodnight. He looked at me and said, "Mommy, tell Grandpa to go to bed too."

"Why?" I asked. "It's not his bedtime yet."

Alex said, "He's tired and angry and he needs some sleep to feel better."

I had to laugh to myself. I told Alex, "You know, buddy, you weren't very nice to Grandpa at dinner and so he had every right to get upset with you, and Daddy and I had every right to give you consequences for your behavior."

Just when I wasn't sure he even understood what I had just said to him, he responded, "But I lost two things—the TV button *and* my ice cream. I didn't like that."

"I know," I said, and kissed him goodnight and left the room.

The next morning Alex was fine and interacted with his grandfather as though nothing had happened the night before. In his mind, the incident was over, he learned his lesson, and he moved on. But my father-in-law was still very upset and Alex could not understand why his grandfather didn't want to talk to him.

This incident, in particular, taught me a poignant lesson. It made me realize how much we learn from each other and how so much of our behavior and reactions are learned by watching others. If only we could all keep the "uncluttered" mind of my son's, we would be so much better off. Nick once told me, early on in Alex's life, that he is a part of this family just like the others. He needs rules and consequences for his misdeeds just like the rest of us. At the time, I was angry and didn't understand how he could be so mean. But, I realized throughout the years how important it has been to give appropriate consequences and not to "give in" to him because we "feel sorry" for him. Although Nick and I can be very overprotective of Alex and his needs, we have come to the mutual agreement that, just like our other children, Alex does occasionally need to be reprimanded.

> We just have to understand, and help others to understand, that although he looks physically older, we need to limit his consequences to reflect his mental capacity.

There's a fine line there, and we are working together to find it.

8

Prepare for the Worst, Hope for the Best

I was pushing my infant daughter, Angela, in her baby swing in our backyard and Alex was playing in the sandbox next to us when my neighbor walked over from her backyard across the way.

"How's Alex doing?" were the first words that came out of her mouth.

"He's okay," was all I managed to say at that moment. The fact that he did suffer some major brain damage from all the seizures ripped through me whenever I thought about it. Mentally, he wasn't the same anymore. We were still reeling from the consequences.

During the five years we lived in New Jersey, my neighbor, who was a nurse, became very dear to me. She was always kind to me and my kids, and always tried to raise my hopes up instead of bringing them down. If you have a friend like that, treasure them, for they are truly a gift from God. I was thankful for her friendship. She always knew what to say and when to say it, and today was no exception.

"You make it look so easy, when I know it isn't easy for you," were the next words that came out of her mouth.

"What do you mean?" I asked her as I continued to push Angela's swing.

"Well, the other morning as my husband and I were finishing breakfast we noticed Nick in the driveway shooting basketballs with

Kellie and Nicholas." She continued, "Then we saw you bring Alex out and sit on the bottom of your driveway and draw with chalk."

"Yeah, well, Alex likes to do that," I responded.

"I know," she said. Then she continued to say that she was touched by watching us interact as a family after all we'd been through. She had three boys of her own, about the same ages as mine, and although times could be trying raising her kids, she knew for me that it was even tougher because I had to deal with Alex's health issues on top of it. She continued to say that she and her husband noticed we looked like a "normal" family.

"Normal" for us was very different from the typical American family. Our lives had limits. Limits because of Alex's seizure activity that could happen anywhere, anytime, and often did. We couldn't take him to the pool to swim unless someone was always right next to him in the water. We couldn't let him jump on the neighbor's trampoline like the rest of the kids, for fear he would overexert himself and go into a seizure. We couldn't let him play in the snow and sled down the hill at the corner. We couldn't let him ride the roller coaster at the local theme park, for fear that he could seize on the ride and injure himself.

> We came to realize that all of the things we thought of as typical were no longer possible, but we tried to live as normal a life as we could for the sake of our other kids.

"You make it look so easy" resonated in my ears as she spoke those words to me. "Well it ain't easy!" was all I wanted to scream back at the time.

"We are learning to adjust our lifestyle to accommodate his needs," was all I said as we continued to talk. "I guess although I don't like what is happening to him, I can't change it."

"How true that is," she said to me, "and I just want you to know that I admire you for how you are handling your situation. We look over here and think what a nice, happy family you have. You and Nick are so involved with your kids and enjoy being with them, and well, I really admire that in you."

"That's very kind of you to say," I responded back for lack of anything else to say to her.

That conversation with my friend often entered my thoughts over the years and it was not long after that, when we took the kids to the beach for a few days, that I thought of my dear friend again. We were staying at a hotel with a pool and went swimming one afternoon with our four kids. Nick was goofing around with the other three while I swam with Alex. Not long into our swim, Alex went into a seizure in the water. Thank goodness I was right next to him and was able to hold his head above the water. Nick, Kellie, Nicholas, and Angela immediately came to our aid. We got Alex to the side of the pool, lifted him out, wrapped him in some beach towels, and laid him on a lounge chair by our things. There was no lifeguard on duty and we'd been through this scenario before, so we just dealt with it as best we knew how. The seizure finally stopped and as all five of us knelt next to him, we said a little prayer of gratitude that he was okay now. He immediately fell asleep, as is usual after he seizes, and we knew he would be out of it for at least an hour. We sat at the picnic table next to him and decided to eat the lunch I had packed while he slept off the seizure. It was as good a time as any to eat our lunch and stay near to observe him as he slept. As we were eating, an older gentleman walked over to us.

"Is your son okay?" he asked.

"Yeah, he'll be fine," Nick responded.

"That's good," he said, and then continued to tell us that he had just witnessed what happened in the pool and how all of us pitched in to help get our son to safety. "I admire and respect each one of you for making it look so easy when I know it ain't."

"Well, we do the best we can. We just want him to be safe and okay," I said. And then he said something to me that I have never forgotten to this day.

"Prepare for the worst, but hope for the best," and he walked away.

"What did he mean by that?" I asked my husband as the man disappeared.

"I'll have to think about that one," Nick said to me, and with a puzzled look on my face I said, "So will I."

Over the years, that man's words have become somewhat of a mantra for our family. Prepare for the worst. We are always prepared, as best we can, when it comes to Alex. We have on hand the Diastat, the drug we give him to stop the seizing should he go into status epilepticus again. We have a soft-shelled helmet to place on his head for long-distance walking on hard surfaces, to break his fall and help prevent his head from splitting open again should he fall into a grand mal seizure. We have a wheelchair handy for the times when we do a lot of walking at the zoo or a theme park or on a nature walk to keep him from overexerting himself. And we all pitch in.

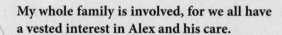

My whole family is involved, for we all have a vested interest in Alex and his care.

We try to anticipate certain patterns in his routine to prevent the seizures from happening, as best we can. We all work together to make our "family life" work.

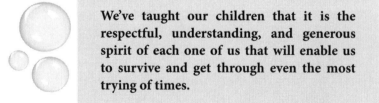

We've taught our children that it is the respectful, understanding, and generous spirit of each one of us that will enable us to survive and get through even the most trying of times.

Although we can't foresee what the future holds, hopefully we are prepared for the worst.

Alex, wearing his soft-shelled helmet.

Hope for the best. We always have that in our minds, hearts, and prayers, especially when it comes to Alex. Without hope, we wouldn't be able to trudge forward and get through some of the difficult days with him. We will always hope for the best!

STAGE THREE

Bargaining...

The stage of grief where you recognize that this is actually happening and you try to negotiate a less painful outcome.

"How can I influence or change what is happening?"

9

Serenity Prayer

"Do you ever think that maybe you are praying for the wrong things?" my dad asked me one Sunday afternoon when we were visiting with the kids for dinner. I looked at him a bit puzzled and he could tell, so he continued, "Well, maybe since you can't change what is happening to Alex, instead of praying for a miracle, you could ask for help in dealing with it. It's a start anyway."

My father is a man of few words. He is a very religious man and when he talks to us about our faith he lets us know how he feels and then wants us to reflect on it for a while. After this conversation with him, I knew I had a lot of thinking, praying, and soul searching to do.

Alex and his grandfather.

I have a plaque that hangs in my family room with one of my favorite prayers on it.

God, grant me the serenity to accept the things I cannot change, courage to change the things I can, and wisdom to know the difference. ~Reinhold Niebuhr

Through the years, this "Serenity Prayer" became a fixture in my talks with God. I slowly began to recognize that what was happening to Alex was out of my control, and although I was always trying to "bargain" with God to make him healthy like my other children, maybe that just wasn't meant to be. Over the years, my dad's words that Sunday afternoon made me see things a lot differently.

> **My prayers soon changed from "How can I change Alex?" to "How can I change my attitude and improve Alex's quality of life?"**

One afternoon as we were driving along the highway, Alex was looking out the window at the scenery. It was a lovely spring day and I had all four children in the car with me.

"Look, Mommy, at all those pretty yellow flowers over there," he said to me as we passed a field full of dandelions.

"Those are weeds," his older sister said to him.

"Yeah," Nicholas piped in, "they are called dandelions."

I laughed to myself at the conversation taking place between my young children.

"But I like them, they are pretty," Alex responded back to his siblings. Alex always sees the beauty in the simplest things. He has such a sense of wonder and appreciates the value of even something most consider an eyesore!

On another occasion, I took the three older kids to a new sibling class offered at our local hospital before Angela, our youngest, was born. The class was supposed to help prepare the kids for the adjustment of having a new baby in the family. At the time, Kellie was seven years old, Nicholas was five and a half, and Alex was four.

The instructor was going to show the kids in the class how to hold an infant properly and get them used to having a new sibling to deal with.

"Pick a baby," she told the children in the class as she pointed to the dolls lined up against the wall. Kellie walked over and picked a baby girl doll, for she wanted a baby sister. Nicholas chose a baby boy doll, for he was hoping for another brother. Alex walked over and picked up an African American baby to use as his prop. Kellie and Nicholas giggled as Nicholas asked his brother, "Why did you pick that one?"

I'll admit I was a bit puzzled at the time too as to why Alex would choose the baby of color, but said nothing. His response to his brother was, "It's a baby." That's all he said—simple as that!

It's a baby. And he was right. She said to pick a baby, and he did. He chose a baby. To him it was no different than the one his brother and sister had picked. Alex didn't see color. He simply saw a baby.

After these incidents I began to realize how little we truly understand about our perception of the world. I've gained this insight from my son. You see, to Alex, that field of "weeds" was a field of "yellow beautiful flowers," and the baby he chose was "just a baby," no different than any other baby. Alex now has three African American cousins. My sister adopted three teenagers from Ethiopia recently and to Alex they are no different than any of his other cousins. He loves them and hugs and embraces them, telling them they are beautiful, for he is a child without judgment or prejudice, who sees past color or physical beauty, and instead looks within and sees a beautiful person.

As the years pass, I have begun to see the world as one I'd never have known if it weren't for Alex. My mother always taught us kids a prayer of her own that I say every morning, to this day, as I awake from bed. After thanking God for the day ahead, I say, "Lord, help me to know that nothing is going to happen to me today that together you and I can't handle." And I know He will.

We may always want to change what is happening to us or wish for a different outcome, but I am a firm believer in the fact that everything happens for a reason, and although we think we know what's best for us, we often do not.

Alex, in all his simplicity, helps our family put life in perspective in ways we never thought possible.

10
Holland vs. Italy

"I just don't know what to tell these parents. I mean, I'm not even a parent myself yet and I surely don't have the answers for these parents of special needs kids." The school social worker, Christy, sighed as she sat down next to me in the faculty lunchroom.

Christy was in her early twenties and we had developed a strong mentoring relationship. Over the school year, she was a comfort to me as I talked about Alex's struggles and issues. I was a resource to her as I helped her understand the emotions and attitudes of the parents she was working with.

Christy continued to tell me about her frustrating morning. A family had come in to the school for a tour. They had two sons. This particular school housed two very different programs. One program was for gifted students in the district and the other was for cognitively impaired students. It was an elementary school for kindergarten through sixth grade. My son attended the special education program here. These particular parents were already very familiar with the gifted program that their eldest son was currently in. Today's visit was for their younger son.

Like Alex, their younger son had suffered some seizures during childhood and had not progressed mentally as rapidly as their older son. They were here to view the cognitively impaired program to determine if it would be a good fit for the younger boy. However, the parents were in denial about their youngest child's impairments. Now that he was of school age, they desperately wanted to place him in the gifted program with their older son. Christy was trying to encourage them to look at the other program because it was a much better fit for their younger boy. After touring the building and program and seeing the other special needs children in the program, they became even more adamant about having their second child in the gifted program.

"He'll be fine and thrive once he gets started, you'll see," they kept telling Christy. Christy tried to reason with them. She was extremely frustrated because she did not know how to get through to them. They insisted that since they are both very intelligent, their boys will be as well. They wouldn't even listen to her and it was so obvious that their youngest boy was impaired.

I looked to Christy and said, "When we realized Alex was not like our other children, I used to wonder what I ever did to deserve this. My other three children were smart and reached all their milestones on schedule. We ignored some of Alex's shortcomings and enrolled him in regular kindergarten thinking he would be fine, he'd come around...and then he got worse as the seizures increased, instead of getting better. As I was 'bargaining' with God to 'cure' him, my brother told me this story:

"A husband and wife were on a plane traveling to Italy. It had been a very long flight and they had just awakened from a deep sleep. The pilot came on the intercom and announced that due to bad weather they had to make a detour and instead of arriving in Italy, they would be landing in Holland. The husband and wife were visibly upset. The airline attendant asked them what was wrong. They proceeded to tell her that they paid to go to Italy and therefore were expecting to go to Italy. They wanted to see Venice and Rome and all the ancient cities and art treasures that Italy had to offer. They would settle for nothing less. The attendant then asked them if they had ever been to Holland. They told her they had not, and she explained that obviously then they didn't know what Holland had to offer. She told them of the beautiful countryside, medieval castles, Gothic churches, windmills, and fields full of tulips that were just some of the highlights that Holland had to offer. Give it a chance, go there with an open mind and no agenda, and you just might enjoy it more than you ever imagined."

"Great story," Christy replied, "and I see how it applies, but will they?"

"Well," I said, "you can use me as an example. I've been in their shoes. I have three intelligent, beautiful children and one that is maybe not as intelligent, but just as beautiful as the others. And although he isn't as 'book smart' as the others, he is teaching the rest of us things we would not otherwise have known—things like compassion and unconditional love, and simplicity and enjoying the moment, and taking nothing for granted. And until I truly realized what he had to offer, I always looked past it wishing for something else.

> You have to open your mind and your heart to what each child has to offer and then you can truly come to terms with them and actually embrace the experience."

"Wow," she said and thanked me for the words of wisdom. As she got up to leave, she turned to me and smiled, "You really should write that book about your experience. I'd buy it."

11
Touching Lives

"Why would God put special needs kids in the world?" my friend asked me one day when I was going through a rough patch with Alex. "It makes me want to cry and I always feel sorry for them."

I knew she was concerned for me and my son, and I knew she hoped she would never be in my shoes having to deal with such issues. But I also realized that because she was only focusing on their needs, she couldn't see past that to learn what they have to offer. It is much easier to complain about what we lack than to be grateful for what we possess.

Special needs kids are *not* put in this world for us to feel sorry for them. If anything, we are feeling sorry for ourselves. They are a product of their circumstances. A traumatic birth, an extra chromosome, an accident, or a serious illness may have led to their "specialness." That cannot be changed. So we must deal with it. And these kids deal with it better than you or I ever could. For the most part, they seem to be the gentlest, kindest, happiest kids I have ever met. They know what is most important and they just want to be loved and cared for like the rest of us. Unlike you and me, they don't need much in life to make them happy. The goals we strive for to attain success and wealth mean nothing to them. A hug, a smile, a kind word, a thumbs-up, or a high-five can thrill them to no end.

So, why do I think God put special needs kids in the world? To touch lives.

I used to dwell on the question, "What is my purpose in life?" Although I realized, in part, it was to be a good wife and mother, I wanted to do more. I became involved in special education and now serve as a substitute teacher. I enjoy it immensely, and why did I do it? Because of Alex.

My daughter, Kellie, is a college student. Throughout high school, as she was applying to college, she struggled with what to study and what to do with her future. One day, she volunteered in one of Alex's classrooms and really liked it. She then asked if she could shadow some of his teachers and staff that service him. She was exposed to teaching, speech therapy, occupational therapy, and physical therapy. My friend likes to say that Alex gave Kellie a career. She decided to pursue a career in occupational therapy and is currently in graduate school earning her master's degree in that field. Why? Because of Alex.

When Alex was a toddler, Nick suggested that we go out on a date. He brought to my attention that we had put our social lives on hold for Alex. Because of Alex's seizures and health problems, I never left his side. But Nick was right. We were still a couple and needed to make time for each other. We would find a good baby-sitter, stay local on our dates, and it would all work out. I interviewed many teenagers in my neighborhood and church. If they weren't comfortable with Alex and his condition, I didn't want them. Finally I found a young teenager named Holly. She turned out to be a godsend to us and babysat for many years for us. She went on to college to pursue a teaching degree in special education. She is now in her thirties with a family of her own and is a special education consultant. Why? Because of Alex.

Nick works for Ford Motor Company, a big supporter of the United Way. We have always given money to this charity, but always wanted to give to a cause that was more personal, where our charitable contributions were being well spent. When Alex was diagnosed with epilepsy, we turned to the Epilepsy Foundation of Michigan to learn more. My husband also wanted to give back to this community that has given us so much support and information through the years. Nick currently serves on the board of directors for the Epilepsy Foundation of Michigan. Our whole family is involved in fundraisers and support groups to raise awareness and to help those with epilepsy lead a productive life. Why? Because of Alex.

My daughter, Angela, is an athlete. Her love of the game of basketball exceeds words. She is always shooting a basketball in our driveway when she gets a free moment. Alex often goes in the driveway to join her and "shoot hoops." Recently Angela had to perform some Christian service hours for one of her classes at school. One recent Saturday, she got the opportunity to volunteer and referee at a Special Olympics basketball tournament at a local high school. She enjoyed the kids very much and wants to continue volunteering in this venue. Why? Because of Alex.

Every Friday night, one of the paraprofessionals from Alex's school organizes a night of bowling for the special education teens at a local bowling alley. It is a great program and Alex looks forward to hanging out with his peers to enjoy bowling, pizza, and fun. On a recent Friday, a pretty senior girl approached me as Alex and I were entering the bowling alley. I did not know this young lady, but obviously Alex did because he immediately gave her a hug and told her she was beautiful. She smiled, thanked him, and turned to me.

"Mrs. Broggi," she said, "Hi, I'm Clarissa. I worked with Alex in one of his classes at the high school." I said hello to her and she continued, "I just need to tell you that your son always makes my day. I can be having a bad day and I come into his class to assist the kids and he always makes me feel better."

"That's very sweet of you to say," I told her.

"It's very true," she went on. "I didn't know what to study at college next year and now I do. I'm going to study to be a special education teacher."

"That's a great field!" I responded.

"I want you to know that it's because of Alex that I made this decision."

Wow, I thought to myself. Why is she going that route? Because of Alex.

Now I have an even better answer for my friend the next time she asks me, "Why would God put special needs kids in the world?" My answer would be, "To change lives."

For that is just what Alex has done!

Depression...

The stage of grief characterized by feelings of hopelessness and inadequacy.

"I really can't deal with what is happening!"

12
The Letter

When we were still living in New Jersey and Alex was about eight years old, he contracted a virus and became very ill. He was hospitalized for a number of days because illness brings seizures for Alex and it was hard to get them under control. He was having many grand mal seizures per day and the doctors were trying to find yet another good mix of anti-epileptic drugs to keep them under control. They finally did and he was released from the hospital. We brought him home, gave the medicines on schedule, and he slept—a lot—on the couch. The seizures were fewer and far between now, but Alex was a "zombie." He hardly moved off the couch, did not interact with us much at all, and had such emptiness in his eyes.

"At least he's not seizing," the neurologist told me when I called with concern.

"But he's not doing much of anything at all!" I wanted to scream back into the telephone. All the drugs may have been suppressing the seizures, but they were also restraining my son from moving forward, and I really couldn't deal with that. I knew I had to pull myself out of this funk I was in, because it wasn't doing my family any good for me, the normally positive and upbeat member of the family, to be depressed.

One afternoon, I called my sister, Maryann, to vent. As I talked, she listened. And then I sobbed into the phone, "I cannot do this anymore. It is so hard and I feel so helpless and hopeless!"

She just listened some more and told me everything would be okay. "Have faith and pray about it," she said. "This too shall pass, and you'll get through it."

I thanked her for listening, hung up the phone, and cried. I went through more than two boxes of tissues. While I was crying, I kept thinking about how I was going to get through this and how I could make my son better.

A few days passed and Alex was still very drugged and lethargic. Nick and I made a decision to look for a different neurologist. We were disappointed that his current doctor only seemed concerned that Alex wasn't seizing. We wanted a better quality of life for him than that. We felt we would search for a neurologist who shared our vision and had the best interest of our son in mind. I actually got excited making phone calls to doctors' offices asking for referrals to the best neurologists in the area.

> As parents, we were our child's best advocate and we were going to see that he got the best possible care.

In the midst of my search a few days later, a letter arrived in my mailbox. It was addressed to me and arrived from Maryann, the sister I called at the peak of my depressed state—the one I thought couldn't possibly understand what I was going through.

Maryann told me that as a young girl she always looked up to me and that she still does. She told me that I make motherhood look so easy even with the trials and tribulations we experience, especially with Alex. She told me that she could think of no one in this entire world that could be a better mother to Alex than I. And she ended her letter telling me how much she loved me and was proud to be my little sister. She then stated that "God knew what he was doing when he blessed you and Nick with Alex."

That letter meant more to me than I could ever express. I read and reread that letter many times. Maryann's words were definitely sinking in and that letter became a turning point for me. I was finally coming to terms with why Alex was given to us.

> **I was so busy focusing on what I wanted him to be that I lost sight of the blessing that he was.**

Not long after that letter, Alex received a card and letter in the mail from his very spiritual grandmother. My mother holds a special place in her heart for all of her grandchildren, but she calls Alex her "sweetheart." He tells her, "Grandma, *you* are the sweetheart!"

Alex and his grandmother.

She prays often for him and his health problems and always tells me "the Lord never gives us more than we can handle." On some of the more difficult days I tell her that He has some pretty high expectations from me and we laugh.

I read and reread the card my mother sent to Alex and I was deeply touched by her heartfelt words:

"May your days be blessed with the knowledge of the special purpose God has for your life. And may you be aware of the blessing you are to so many."

She went on to explain how Alex is a blessing to his family and how much she enjoys spending time with him. The letters from my mom and from my sister made such a difference in my life, and at a time when I really needed it.

I finally realized how much Alex gave my life purpose!

13

Angel in Disguise

I'll be the first to admit that I was having a very difficult time dealing with all the seizures Alex had, and I felt a deep sense of hopelessness. I felt like our lives were on hold. Nick kept reminding me that, as Alex's parents, we were his best advocates and we needed to do everything we could to help get him better. And so we did. You name it, we tried it.

We learned that epilepsy cannot be cured, but it can eventually go away or be outgrown. This gave us hope. If only the seizures would go away, he could learn and go on to lead a productive and normal life. We researched all our options and explored each one.

Medication is the most common form of treatment, or management, for those with epilepsy. You name the anti-epileptic drug, and we tried it. These drugs typically block the seizure from spreading, not necessarily stop it from initiating. According to the Epilepsy Foundation, approximately 15-40% of people with epilepsy fail to gain control of their seizures despite optimal medical management. That seems to be where Alex falls. We do not have control. He is currently on a good mix of drugs that have given him the best control we've seen in years.

Medical management of epilepsy is very important. The most common forms of management are the use of medications, which we currently employ; the ketogenic diet, which did not work for

Alex; the vagus nerve stimulator, which we opted not to try for many reasons; and surgery, which is often a last resort and one we definitely considered.

Alex was admitted to the hospital just shy of his tenth birthday as we explored the surgery option. We were told that if the doctors could pinpoint the portion of the brain that is causing the seizures, it could be removed, thus preventing them from occurring. We were desperate at least to see if he was a candidate for such a procedure.

He was admitted to the hospital, electrodes were attached to his head, and seizures were induced to see if they could determine where they were starting. He was in the hospital for about a week as they monitored him.

> We were determined to do everything in our power to get our son better.

One evening as Alex was quietly sleeping, I strolled down the hallway of the hospital peering into the other kids' rooms and wondering why they were admitted. As I passed by one room, I noticed a middle-aged woman sitting by her son's bedside knitting as he slept. She had a pair of reading glasses sitting on her nose and she glanced over to me as she saw me look her way.

"Hi," she said, trying to grab my attention. "Can I help you?"

I didn't know how to respond at first, so I walked into the room.

"Do you need something?"

"Oh, no," I said. "My son is down the hall and I'm just taking a walk while he sleeps."

"Is everything okay?" she asked. "You seem a little down."

I then proceeded to tell her why my son was in the hospital and how he has a lot of seizures and so we were considering brain surgery to stop them. I told her that I was scared at the thought of it, but we didn't have any other options left. She listened very intently to every word, and she said to me, "I can't imagine what you are going through. That must be so hard for you to watch your son having seizures. I will pray for you and your son and I know, with the Lord's help, you will make the best decision for him."

I was blown away. First of all, where did she come from, why did she care about me and my problems, and why would she want to pray for us when she didn't even know us? Then I felt a little uneasy for telling her all that I was going through and wondered what she was going through herself with her son. Surely it couldn't be as bad as my situation.

"Thank you," I responded kindly. "I appreciate your thoughts and prayers." Then I asked her why she was here and she told me how she was waiting for a kidney transplant for her son. She was very serious and sympathetic. She seemed to perceive my situation as more dire than hers, and I realized that my problems with Alex seemed small compared to what she must be going through. If her son didn't get a kidney, he could surely die, and I just wanted my son to stop having seizures.

That night in the hospital was an eye opener for me. I prayed about her and for her and her son, and

> **I realized that, although my cross can often seem a big burden, others carry larger ones.**

I stopped feeling sorry for myself from that moment on. I truly realized that angels do exist and they look out for us.

Alex ended up not being a candidate for surgery, since the doctors could never pinpoint where the seizures started. We were okay with that, and it actually made our decision an easy one. I was actually glad we were not opting to remove a portion of his brain.

> **I also knew that he would be okay no matter what the future held for him.**

That "angel in disguise" made me see that, and to this day I am grateful for that encounter.

14

Pity Party

Christmas time and birthdays ranked as some of my favorite times of the year. After all, who doesn't enjoy a celebration? Alex, too, loves both of these holidays and not at all for the exchanging of gifts involved. He loves to get together with family, friends, and loved ones to celebrate. But unfortunately, as much as I looked forward to these events, I also began to dread them.

Alex thrives on routine. In order to keep his health in balance and the seizures at bay, we must strive to keep him on a schedule. He needs to get at least ten hours of sleep per night, he needs to take his antiseizure medications at the same time three times a day, and most of all, he needs to be kept calm and peaceful as much as possible. Any major changes to his schedule or agitation or overexertion are likely to cause a seizure. This isn't an easy way to live, but we try our best to stick to his rigid schedule. And when we don't or can't, problems are sure to arise.

Christmas time at my parents' house is fun, chaotic, and crazy all at the same time. I am one of eight children and we all get together with our spouses and children to celebrate on Christmas Eve.

For the past nineteen years, since Alex has come into our lives, this time of year for us has always been filled with seizures. We can almost guarantee that he will have at least one, sometimes more, during the holidays. His routine is thrown out of whack, he doesn't get the rest he needs, and the excitement of the season adds to the situation. One of my nieces or nephews will come yelling up the stairs for Aunt Joan and Uncle Nick to "come quick, because Alex is seizing." As much as we try to prevent this from happening, it almost always does. So we deal with it. The kids all quickly learned the routine—clear the area, loosen his shirt at the neck, get a cool compress to place on his forehead so he doesn't overheat, and call Nick or me to the room. Although this scenario had become too routine, it was never easy and we did not like dealing with it. We hated that Alex's seizures put a damper on the festivities.

Should we have just stayed home and skipped the holidays? we would ask ourselves. *And was that fair to our other kids? Was that fair to our extended family? Was it fair to us? Was it fair to Alex?*

Nick always used to tell me that we can't stop living, and he was right. We'd take the necessary precautions and leave the rest to God. If it was going to happen, we'd deal with it and do so to the best of our ability.

Birthday parties were a similar risk, although on a much smaller scale. Alex always wanted to have his birthday party at home with a few friends, his siblings, a few cousins, and close family friends. He usually wanted pizza and cake and he always wanted a piñata filled with candy for the guests to help him break open and enjoy the treats inside.

Alex at his birthday party.

For Alex's fourteenth birthday party, Angela asked if she could invite her good friend, Maura. I agreed, and her nine-year-old friend arrived with a large gift in hand. Alex was excited, trying to guess what she got him. After we ate pizza, we went outside to take turns hitting the piñata with a stick to break it open. When it was Alex's turn, he spun around, trying too hard to hit the piñata, and must have made himself dizzy because down he went to the grass falling into a grand mal seizure. We all came to his aid as his body twitched and jerked for about five minutes. After the seizure ended, we got him safely inside. We laid him on the family room couch to sleep it off for about an hour or so. Once he was safe and resting, we resumed the party. Nick went outside to finish the piñata with the kids and I stayed in the kitchen to clean up and keep an eye on Alex as he slept nearby. My mom, friend, and sisters joined me at the kitchen table as we talked and laughed amongst ourselves.

Unbeknownst to me at the time, Maura was taking in everything. After the party, Angela told me that Maura asked her a lot of questions about what happened to Alex and wondered if he would be okay. Angela felt she answered all of Maura's questions and that Maura was satisfied. Evidently she did not, because later that evening, Maura's mom called me. She was a friend of mine and knew a little bit about Alex and his seizures, and she was calling to see if he was okay. I assured her that he was and thanked her for the SpongeBob pillow she had sent over for Alex.

"He loved it," I told her. Then she told me how Maura couldn't believe that after Alex had the seizure we all went back to laughing and having a good time. My friend assured Maura that we made sure Alex was safe, but since he was going to sleep afterward, what else should we have done?

"I don't know," Maura told her mom, "Maybe they could have cried. I know I wanted to."

I did get choked up a bit but had to laugh, for I knew she was just as curious as Maura.

"You know," I said to her, "we have dealt with many, many seizures that Alex has had over the past fourteen years of his life, more than I ever care to add up. I've had the 'pity parties' through the years, more than I care to admit.

> **I decided, along with my husband, that we aren't doing anybody else in this family any good when we wallow in self-pity.**

We have decided that this is the hand we have been dealt, and we will play our cards the best we know how. So we deal with it, make sure he is okay, and move on. We really don't have any other choice."

When Alex would wake up from his rest period after the seizure, mostly he would remember the good time he was having before it happened. He often didn't recall or even talk about the actual seizure. Either he couldn't remember it happening, or he just didn't want to dwell on it. And neither did we. As he got older, he would say, "I didn't like the way that made me feel and made me fall down," and we would acknowledge the same and move on.

"No need to dwell on something we are unable to fix" soon became our motto.

Acceptance...

The stage of grief where you begin to see the upside and regain a sense of control.

"I will deal with what is happening and make the best of it."

15
Attitude is Everything

Ialways thought I was the one in our family with the most positive attitude. That was until I met my son.

There's a joke in our family that Mom always has a half-full cup and Dad's is always half empty. My kids bring this up often, especially to their father, who prefers to view it more as, "I'm the 'realistic' one in the family and Mom likes to live in the 'fantasy' world."

Recently, we were staying at a beautiful condo resort in Orlando, Florida, over my children's Easter break from school. The older two could not join us on this trip due to their college schedules, so we were there with Angela, a freshman in high school, and Alex, a senior in special education in high school.

We had just spent Sunday at the beach and Monday at Sea World and were taking the picture-perfect, sunny, eighty-degree weather for granted.

We awoke on Tuesday morning with plans to attend yet another theme park in the area when we looked out the window to see gray skies and pouring rain. We turned on the Weather Channel only to find out that this weather was going to continue throughout the entire day, and that there was even a tornado watch in the vicinity.

"Bummer!" shouted Angela from her comfy bed as she tossed a pillow at her brother Alex.

"Stop that!" he giggled as he threw it back at her.

"This sucks," my husband stated in disgust as he looked out the window. "Now what are we going to do today?"

Always looking for the humor in most situations, I piped in, "Well, we could sit in this hotel room all day and stare at each other!" My husband just looked at me, and Alex started giggling.

"It's okay," Alex said. "We're in Florida!" And he was right about that—we had just left thirty-five-degree temperatures in Michigan and this heat was simply divine to us. "Anyway," he continued, "the coconut trees need the water."

I knew that no matter how hard we tried, we could not control the weather—so why freak out about it? We just needed to make the best out of the situation.

That day, my husband pulled out his laptop and proceeded to weed through the hundreds of e-mails that would have been waiting for him when he returned to work the following week. Angela went over to her friend's large condo near ours. She spent the day hanging out with a friend she doesn't get to spend much time with back home because they attend different high schools. And Alex and I lay on the large queen bed in our room with stacks of pillows beneath our heads watching cartoons on TV. As we watched a show about a pig family, he snuggled up his six foot, two inch frame next to me and lay his head on my shoulder.

"Mommy," he said to me, "you are beautiful."

I was moved by the pureness of his words, because in my heart I knew how much he meant what he was saying. He wasn't into my physical appearance at all, for I had just woken up, bed head and all, and was hardly a pretty sight. He was just so very grateful to be spending some quality time with his mother, watching a silly television show, and giggling together.

> Nothing else in the world mattered to him, except that he was sharing time with me and his father in a small hotel room as the rain poured outside the window.

Had we been home and it was raining out, I would have been doing any of a hundred other things inside the house besides bonding with my son. I realized as we were watching mindless television, laughing, and cuddling, we were truly enjoying each other's company.

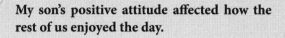

My son's positive attitude affected how the rest of us enjoyed the day.

16

The Airport

Nick grew up on one of the lakes in Michigan. His parents owned a home on a canal that led out to Lake St. Clair. They owned a boat and Nick spent many summer days boating and fishing with his parents and siblings. He always dreamed of sharing those happy memories with his own family someday.

When we first got married and started a family, I chose to stay home and raise our children. Without two incomes, we realized our dream of owning a home on the water was distant. As the years passed, we talked about buying a small cottage in Northern Michigan someday where we could take the kids to boat and fish. Financially, we could not afford the cottage because we chose to spend our money on private Catholic education for our kids instead. Eventually, we did purchase a boat that we still store at a marina and enjoy taking out on Lake Erie to water-ski and fish with the kids. We've done this for the past several years and enjoy it immensely.

But, the yearning to live on the water has never left Nick, and because we saved a few dollars over the years, we started discussing purchasing a small home on the water again. We have decided to look south this time instead of north; Alex handles the warmer weather much better than the cold.

Nick and I have flown to Florida chasing the dream of owning a waterfront home with a built-in pool for Alex and a fishing dock for

Nick—somewhere the three of us can retire to someday and enjoy life. I can picture Nick on the dock, a fishing pole in one hand and a beer in the other, casting a pole until the sun sets. I see Alex, with his life vest on to always keep him afloat in the event of a seizure, splashing around in the cage-covered pool off the back of our house, and me sitting poolside with one eye on Alex and the other lost in a book. I can't wait for the other kids, and their future spouses and our future grandchildren, to visit us on their breaks from school and work.

Coming home from another unsuccessful house-hunting venture, we were at the Detroit Metropolitan Airport waiting for our luggage to arrive. As Nick and I stood there waiting, I noticed an older couple standing near the conveyor belt with their son. The couple appeared to be in their mid to late fifties and their son, who seemed to have special needs himself, looked to be in his late twenties. He had "raccoon eyes," like the ones Alex gets from wearing his sunglasses in the Florida sun. The circles around his eyes appeared white and the rest of his face had a sunkissed glow to it. I laughed and thought of Alex as I studied this young man. As the luggage entered the belt, the father motioned to his wife to come help get their luggage. She turned to her son, whispered to him, and smiled as she walked away and went to help her husband. The young man smiled back at her and waited there patiently as his parents unloaded their luggage from the belt.

Nick was watching me and smiled at me. As we walked away with our own luggage, he said to me, "So were you thinking what I was when you saw that couple with their special needs son?"

"Probably," I responded. "I was thinking that will be us with Alex someday, escaping to our Florida house to enjoy some R&R until you retire."

"Exactly," he smiled at me.

And in that moment I felt a huge sense of relief overcome me, for I now knew that my husband and I had finally totally accepted and embraced our situation with Alex. We both knew that it wouldn't be just Nick and me retiring to Florida and spending our golden years together. It would be the three of us, and it would be just as wonderful.

17

Live Simply, But Live Right

My son wants for very little in life. The things that excite him are so very simple. A smile, a kind word, a hug— these are the very things that make his day and mean the world to him. We call him the "charmer" because he knows how to make somebody else's day too by these simple gestures. "You're beautiful," he will tell someone, and not necessarily because of their physical appearance, but because of who they are. He can read people pretty well and sense if they are good inside and out, and he often tells them so.

> Alex knows right from wrong, and I've come to realize he knows this better than I do, and he always applies it to his life as well as mine.

When my youngest daughter, Angela, was a freshman in high school, she played on the varsity basketball and soccer teams. She is a talented athlete, and as much as I would like to claim that she gets it from me, I think she truly developed her athletic abilities watching her older siblings play and learning from them all those years she was dragged to their games. Twice a week, the days after her games, I would go to the newsstand box in front of the gas station near her school to get the local paper with the results of the games from the previous day.

On one particular day, I was excited to get the paper on my way with Alex to pick her up from school. The night before, Angela had a game-high twenty points and ten rebounds (a double-double) and was named the player of the game. I was so proud of her, knowing how well she played to lead her team to a victory, and that she was the youngest player on the court, too. I went to the newsstand, put in my fifty cents, and pulled two newspapers from the pile.

Unbeknownst to me at that time, Alex was watching my every move from his seat in the car. I sat down in the car and quickly opened the paper to the sports section to read about the game and see what was written about Angela. Alex looked right at me and said, "Mommy, you took two papers."

Not really paying attention, I looked back at him and said, "Yeah, look, Angela is in the paper for helping her team win her game!"

"But Mommy," he persisted, "you only paid for one paper. Why did you take two? That's stealing!"

He totally caught me off guard at that moment and I knew he was absolutely right. At that point I was already driving away from the gas station. "I guess you are right, Alex," I said. "I wanted to get a copy of the paper to show Angela and her team and one to keep for her scrapbook."

But he didn't care. "Mommy," he repeated, "if you want two papers, you have to pay for two papers." How right he was and how ashamed I felt. I went back to the newsstand where the delivery man was filling another box.

"Here's fifty cents," I said to him as I handed him the two quarters in my hand.

"Thank you," he said and started to hand me a paper.

"I already took one," I said, and got back into my car and drove away, watching the puzzled look on his face in my rearview mirror. Alex smiled at me as we drove off, and I knew I had done the right thing because of him.

A few years later, I was a substitute teacher for special education kids in my son's school district. I can thank Alex for helping me find one of my callings in life, for I thoroughly enjoy my job working with such awesome kids.

Every Wednesday, our parish priest, Father John, teaches a Bible study class for parishioners and anyone that would like to attend. On the Wednesdays that I am not called into work, I enjoy attending these classes. They are very informative, insightful, and often applicable to the things going on in my life, sometimes more so than I can imagine.

On a recent Wednesday, Father John was reiterating to the class about speaking the truth. "Do not lie," he told us.

As simple as that sounds, it is not always easy to adhere to. In a single day, if we really pay attention to our actions, we can find ourselves unable to follow this very simple rule. I know that I, for one, am guilty of this more than I care to admit. For the most part, I always try to tell the truth and teach my kids to do likewise, but sometimes without even realizing I do it. I lie!

This was particularly true the evening after this Bible study class. And of all people, my special needs son brought it to my attention.

It was getting dark outside and I went to bring our dog in from her kennel behind the garage. I opened the door from the garage into the mud hall and let her inside. Immediately, she tore off and ran through the kitchen.

"Jerzi!" I yelled to her, "Come here!"

She did not listen to me. I was trying to contain her behind the gate in the mud hall so that she wouldn't drag the dirt on her paws through the kitchen. She kept running around the island in the center of the kitchen, and I kept calling her name to no avail.

"Jerzi, come now!" I repeated in a stern voice.

Then I softened. "I have a treat for you," I said, hoping that would entice her to come to me. She finally did come, and as I closed the gate to secure her behind it, I saw Alex watching me to see if I would give her a treat. I did not even have one in my hand at the moment, so I said to him, "I tricked her!"

"You lied to her," he said, in a half-angry voice. "It's not nice to lie!"

I felt horrible. "You're right," I said. "I should not lie."

I went into the pantry and pulled out a dog treat for Jerzi. "I'm sorry Alex," I said to him as I handed the treat to the dog. "You are right. It is not nice to lie."

Gosh, I thought, the things my son teaches me!

18

The Ride of My Life

There are only nineteen months between Alex and his older brother, Nicholas. They share a brotherly bond that is more protective from Nicholas' end. My older son always looks out for his little brother, who is now taller and bigger than him. When Nicholas invites friends over to hang out, he always introduces Alex to them and encourages his brother to shake their hands. Of course, Alex would rather give them a hug, but Nicholas is teaching him how to be appropriate as he gets older. Nicholas never seems to be embarrassed by his brother. Annoyed at times, yes, but embarrassed, not really. He has really accepted him for who he is.

> He just wishes everyone else could see past his brother's impairments and truly recognize the value of his life.

A couple of summers ago, we took a weekend family trip to an amusement park with our children. As they all get older, I treasure any time I can steal them away from their friends and techno gadgets, if even for a few days, so all six of us can just be together and enjoy each other's company as a family. It was a warm, sunny Saturday morning and the first thing we did was rent a wheelchair for Alex for the day. Although he doesn't necessarily ride in it all day, we always rent one for him when there is a lot of walking involved. "Jump in, buddy!" Nicholas told his brother as he wheeled the chair over near him.

"I can't jump," Alex said back to him. Nicholas laughed and took on his role of wheeling his brother through the park for the day. He usually makes a game of it, humoring his brother along the way. It is rather cute to observe, from a mother's perspective, and I've always enjoyed watching their interactions with each other.

We were enjoying our day going on the rides with Alex that he could go on and taking turns sitting with him when he couldn't ride something. It was almost lunchtime and we were all getting hungry when Nick noticed a burger stand.

"Want to eat?" he asked us and in unison, we all responded, "Yes!"

He walked towards the line and asked us what we wanted to order. We were all busy looking up at the menu board above the cashier. We each told him our orders and then he turned to Nicholas. "What do you want?" he said.

Not really thinking, Nicholas let go of the handles of the wheelchair he was gripping and proceeded, for a brief moment, to walk nearer to his father to get a better glimpse of the menu. At that moment, Alex and the wheelchair took off! We were at the top of a small hill with a somewhat steep incline, and Alex rolled down. All five of us noticed him rolling and started running after him.

"What were you thinking? Why did you let go?" Nick and I were yelling to Nicholas as we chased Alex down the hill. The wheelchair rolled about twenty feet, jumped over a small curb, and ended up in a small patch of nicely landscaped flowers. We ran to Alex, who was thankfully still in the wheelchair, albeit not exactly sitting upright. Nick reached him first, and after making sure he was okay, propped him back up on the seat of the chair. We were all clearly upset, Nicholas especially, but glad Alex was okay.

"What happened, buddy?" I asked him as I gave him a hug. "Are you okay? We were so worried you'd fall out and hurt yourself!" I continued to say.

Alex just looked at me with the biggest smile on his face and said, "I'm okay, are you okay? That was fun!"

We all burst into laughter at his remarks and, after making sure all was well, continued with our day.

A short while later we decided to take the kids to the water area of the park to finish our day. Although the kids loved this, I am always nervous with Alex around water. He absolutely loves to swim and so do I, but he needs one-on-one attention constantly whenever he is in or near water. Not only is the risk of drowning a scare because he cannot swim, but the extreme change in temperature from the heat to the cool pool water can cause him to seize. Nick and I try to let him do what the other kids do and enjoy the simple things, like swimming, but it almost always turns out ugly for Alex. And today was no exception.

I was sitting on the lounge chair next to Alex as he blew bubbles I brought from home. Nick was in the wave pool with the other three kids. After a short while, Alex noticed how much fun they were having and wanted to join them. I kept trying to talk him out of it and have him just enjoy his bubbles, but he was persistent. Finally, I gave in to him. After all, it was a very warm day and if I eased him into the water it should be alright for a little while, I thought to myself.

I walked Alex to the edge of the pool and Nick noticed us and came over to assist me with him. "Just for a little bit," I said, and Nick nodded his head.

For about the next ten minutes, Alex was laughing and enjoying the waves in the pool with his siblings. It was surely a wonderful sight to behold. He didn't get to do this very often. All six of us were enjoying our time with him in the waves, when BAM, out of the blue, he went down into the water into a grand mal seizure. Thank goodness, Nick was next to him and caught him as he fell.

The next twenty minutes or so were quite a blur. Alex had a five-minute seizure. We got him safely onto a blanket, wrapped him in a beach towel, and then had him transported to the first aid station in the park where he rested and slept for the next two hours. We opted out of having him taken to the local hospital. We often do, unless the situation becomes more life threatening. We've gotten very good at making this decision. Sitting for several hours in an unfamiliar hospital to run the standard tests and ask us the same questions over and over—we feel it is not always necessary. I stayed with Alex at the first aid station and read while he slept. Nick and the other three kids enjoyed the water park for a couple more hours.

> This was not our ideal situation, but we've learned over the years to live with it and make the best of it.

When Alex awakened a few hours later, he was pretty low key and lethargic. He stayed awake until bedtime, went to bed as normal, and woke up the next day with a fresh start.

The next day we were all enjoying lunch at a fast food restaurant before we began our trip home. As was usual before we left a vacation spot, I asked each member of the family to tell me a high point and a low point of their trip. Each of my children named one of the roller coasters as their high point and Alex having a seizure at the water park as their low point of the trip. I then turned to Alex, trying to put it into a context he would understand and said, "What was your favorite ride at the amusement park?"

Without hesitating, he looked at me and said, "My wheelchair ride!"

"What?" I asked, not quite sure if he understood what I meant.

"I liked going for a ride in my wheelchair down the hill. That was fun!" We all burst into laughter, almost in unison. This made him smile. To think that was the highlight of his trip was amusing to us.

"Okay," I continued, "What was the worst thing about the trip?"

"Nothing," he simply stated.

"You mean your seizure wasn't the low point?" I asked.
"Nope!" he answered.

> At that moment, I thought to myself, how could I ever wish he was anything other than who he was? He has taught his parents and siblings more about compassion and optimism than we ever could have imagined.

Sure, the hardships and health issues with him are very trying and we've had to make many adjustments in our lives with him as a result. But the joy and laughter he's brought into our world exceeds words.

Joy . . .

**For me, looking at the positive in this situation,
gaining a new perspective, and embracing it without fear.**

**"I know everything
is going to be
(better than) okay!"**

19

The Definition

Joy is defined in the *Webster's New World Dictionary* as "a very glad feeling; happiness; great pleasure; delight." I can only say that I have experienced all of the above raising my son.

> **He has brought so much joy to our lives, and he has defined unconditional love and compassion far better than a dictionary ever could have.**

Although joy does not fall into the stages of grief we often hear about, I find it necessary to add to my list because it has become the final stage for me on this journey with my special needs son, and it is an emotion I could have never imagined would apply.

Alex is such an innocent child with an uncomplicated mind, and although he lacks a formal education, he always seems to know the right thing to do. As we go through life, we learn through textbooks, experiences, and other people's actions and behaviors. Some of it is good, to be sure, but some of it is not good and not always right.

> **If we never learned an improper behavior or response or act as a child, we would not pass it on to others.**

In his great simplicity of life he has brought perspective and clarity to mine and has truly become an inspiration.

20

Jumping for Joy

It was a beautiful fall day. The leaves were changing colors, the air was crisp, and I was preparing to plant some bulbs to await next spring's arrival. Alex was outside with me doing one of his favorite activities in the whole world—blowing bubbles. He was about ten years old at the time and was sitting on a lawn chair in the driveway blowing bubble after bubble into the cool air.

"Mommy, what are you doing?" he asked me as I gathered the bulbs, garden gloves, shovel, and knee pads in my hands to begin my planting.

"I'm gonna plant some bulbs," I said to him.

He giggled and said, "Silly mommy, you can't plant light bulbs in the dirt. They go in the lamp."

I laughed because he was right and I was proud of the correlation he had just made. "No, Alex, these are flowers and they will bloom in the spring," I said. "Wanna help me?" I asked him.

"Nope," he replied, "that's not my job."

This was always Alex's answer when he didn't want to do something. And I sincerely believe he thought it wasn't his job either. Right now, his job was to continue blowing his bubbles and enjoying every minute of it. That's what he did.

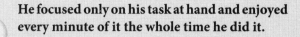

He focused only on his task at hand and enjoyed every minute of it the whole time he did it.

I went over to the area I had designated and began digging holes for my bulbs. About ten minutes into my digging and planting, I noticed Alex was not sitting in his lawn chair anymore. I heard some noise in the garage and went to see what he was up to. He had run out of bubbles and was trying to lift the big refill container off the shelf.

"Need help, buddy?" I asked and went over to assist him. "You have to ask for help when you need it," I reminded him gently.

Alex will not ask for help. He'll try to do it himself or move on to something else, so we always try to encourage him to ask when he needs help.

As I was refilling his little orange non-spill bubble container, a jump rope fell from the shelf. I wasn't paying attention and the next thing I knew, Alex had the jump rope in his hands and was standing in the driveway with it. One hand was grasping each handle and the rope was falling around his feet. I got extremely nervous because he was on the cement, ready to jump. My heart skipped a beat as I looked his way. His soft-shelled helmet, that he should be wearing when on hard surfaces, was nowhere in sight. Before I could get to him or even get the words out of my mouth, he twirled the rope over his head, made it stop at his feet, and then stepped over it.

"What are you doing?" I screamed. He looked at me, startled at my reaction, and simply stated, with a huge smile on his face, "I'm jumping, Mommy. Jumping for joy."

I could not believe the words that had just come out of his mouth. Although he was ten years old, mentally he was about four or five years old. Where had he ever heard that expression before? I had never heard him talk like that. His vocabulary was very limited. I walked over to him and he handed me the jump rope, sat in his lawn chair, and proceeded to blow the bubbles I had just filled for him.

I walked down the driveway to continue planting and tears welled in my eyes. At that very moment, a sense of euphoria filled my heart. It was indescribable and yet so very real. I was filled with joy...absolute joy!

21

Bubbles

It was Christmas morning and Alex was about thirteen years old. Nick was in the kitchen making some coffee and the kids and I were gathered around the Christmas tree sorting through the presents that Santa had left the night before. Angela, our youngest daughter, was eight years old and on the verge of not believing in Santa anymore. She was discussing her doubt with her two older siblings, Kellie and Nicholas, when Alex piped in, "Santa is real, 'cause he brought us all these presents!" The kids and I erupted into laughter. Alex will always believe in Santa, no matter what anyone says otherwise.

Nick joined us in the family room. As is our Christmas morning tradition, we proceeded to open gifts one at a time, from youngest to oldest child. First, Angela opened a gift and we all oohed and aahed and then it was Alex's turn. Alex had a small stack of gifts in front of him, but proceeded to open the smallest one first. It was wrapped in the shape of the bubble maker he had asked for, and he must have known that's what it was. He opened the present before him and shouted, "It's bubbles! Yay, Santa brought me bubbles!"

He was so genuinely happy that it made us all smile. We continued to open the rest of the gifts, and as Alex continued to open presents, he said, "All I wanted was bubbles, but Santa brought me more! He's so nice!" When he said that, I got choked up. For you see, the only thing Alex wrote on his Christmas wish list that year was bubbles. That's all he wanted and he would have been totally content if that was all he got. Such a simple gift meant so much.

Alex has always loved to blow bubbles. He will sit for hours on the patio and blow them. One day, my neighbor was pulling into her driveway after a hectic day of kids and schedules and carpools. She was exhausted and a bit irritated by the day's events. As she pulled down our street, she saw the bubbles floating through the air from our driveway. She knew it was Alex and it brought a huge smile to her face. The problems that day seemed to melt away as she pulled into her driveway next door and saw "the happiest kid I know, enjoying the simplest task."

22
Roots and Wings

"After the skill center, I'm going to go to Michigan State and you're going to miss me," Alex stated out of the blue while I was helping him get ready for bed.

"Really?" I said. "Can I come with you?"

"Nope," he said. "I'm gonna get a roommate like Nicholas."

Amused, I asked him, "When do you think you'll be able to go there?"

"When I stop having seizures," he answered back.

When Alex asks about certain rites of passage such as getting his driver's license and driving a car, Nick and I tell him these things can't happen until he feels better and stops having seizures. We have always felt that although we want to give him hope, we have to be realistic in the process.

"Well, I really will miss you if you go. Are you sure I can't come too?" I asked.

"Nope!" was his answer.

Alex just adores his "big family," as he calls us. He loves when we are all together enjoying each other's company. When his two older siblings left for college, he didn't like it at all. "Why does Kellie have to leave her big family all the time?" he'd say when she would return to college after the summer or a holiday break.

"Nicholas belongs at home with you and me and Daddy and Angela," he said when his brother left for college.

As the years passed, he got used to the idea that they had to go away to learn, but he never liked it. Soon, he wanted to be just like them and go to college.

After high school, Alex will continue his special education program at a place called a "skill center." Michigan law mandates that he attend this center from ages eighteen to twenty-six. At the skill center he will be taught Community-Based Instruction. He will go into the community with his teachers and aides and be taught how to shop for groceries and clothes. He will be taught how to make change so as not to be taken advantage of. In one of the areas of the center there is an apartment. There, he will be taught how to vacuum, keep the apartment clean, make his bed, and do the dishes properly so that maybe one day he can live on his own.

In the laundry class, he will be taught how to sort clothes, use the washing machine, measure soap, use the dryer, and fold clothes. In the kitchen class, he will be taught how to butter bread, make a sandwich, cut a cucumber, and use the microwave. In the personal hygiene class, he will be taught how to brush his teeth properly, use dental floss, take a shower, put on deodorant, and trim his nails. In the greenhouse, he will be taught how to plant flowers, water them, care for them, and watch them grow.

These are just a few of the "life skills" he will learn over the six or seven years of his life following his high school graduation. These skills will help him become more independent. I've tried to tell him that the skill center is his college but he disagrees.

"No, Mommy," he repeats. "After the skill center, I will go to Michigan State."

I've done some substitute teaching at the skill center over the years and I *know* I've learned more from this special education population than they've learned from me. One of my teacher friends once said to me, "These kids are sent to us to be taught, but they are the ones doing the teaching." How true this is!

We all have dreams, goals, and aspirations in life. So does Alex. He wants to achieve his dreams and feel important and do what his older siblings are doing.

> It is necessary, I feel, for him to have a sense of pride, a sense of accomplishment, and a sense of joy to be all he can be.

And I, as his mother, would never discourage him from believing he can accomplish anything he wants to in life. I've always told each of my children that I owe them roots and wings. Why should Alex be any different?

23

Enjoy the Moment

One evening, Nick and I walked into the kitchen from an early evening out. Alex was very excited, pacing around the family room and pointing out the window. He heard the garage door open and was frantically calling to me as I entered the kitchen.

"Mommy, Mommy! Look!" he screamed with excitement as he pointed to the backyard. "Two bunnies! Look, there are two bunnies in our backyard!"

"Wow," I said to him matter-of-factly as I noticed the two cute little bunnies hopping across our backyard.

"Oh, my gosh," he yelled again. "Look there's another one! Now there are three!"

I decided to join in his excitement and said, "Oh my goodness, Alex, there are three beautiful bunnies playing in our backyard. Look at them, they are so cute! I wonder if there are more back there."

"I know, I know!" He couldn't contain his excitement.

His two sisters, previously oblivious to what was happening in the family room because they were playing the piano in the other room, came running in when they heard all of the shouting taking place.

"Hi, Mom," Kellie said. "What's going on in here?"

"Look!" Alex yelled excitedly once again as he pointed to the bunnies outside the window. "There are two, no, three bunnies in our backyard! They are so cute!"

We all started laughing! We were all truly enjoying the moment—my special needs son, my two daughters, myself, and my husband who had just entered the room.

The unbelievable thrill of Alex seeing something so simple as a couple of rabbits jumping around our backyard and the absolute joy it was bringing him to not only witness them but to share it with others was almost beyond comprehension. How can he get so excited about something as simple as this and make it such a wonderful experience for all of us to embrace? Why can't we all be like him in these moments?

> **Why can't we always see the beauty in nature, like he does, and enjoy it to the extreme, like he does?**

Do we take it for granted? Do we not take time, in our busy and hectic lives, to stop and smell the roses? And why don't we? There is really no excuse for why we can't. Alex teaches me that daily.

The next day, we were at the Detroit Zoo, participating in the annual Summer Stroll for Epilepsy, a three-mile walk we attend every year with family and friends. The walk is sponsored by the Epilepsy Foundation of Michigan to help those individuals who have epilepsy and to raise awareness across Michigan. It's a wonderful fundraiser that supports a cause we've embraced because of our son.

*The Broggis participating in the Detroit Zoo's
Summer Stroll for Epilepsy.*

As we began our stroll through the zoo, Alex was so excited! He had gotten a new digital camera for his graduation from some dear family friends, and he couldn't wait to take pictures of all the animals and sights he would see along the way. As we approached the tiger exhibit, he got very excited. Tigers are one of his favorite animals. There were two tigers roaming on the rocks in the distance and Alex hurried over to them, camera in hand, to get a closer view.

"Where are you going, buddy?" I called after him as he swiftly walked to the furthest edge of the fence to get the closest look.

"I want to take a picture of the tiger," he said.

As I followed him, he took the picture, viewed it on his camera, and then just stood there, watching the tiger again.

"What are you doing?" I asked. "Come on, let's catch up to the others; there's lots more to see!"

But he didn't budge. He just stood there and stared at the tiger, taking it all in.

"I really like tigers. They are my favorite animals at the zoo!"

"I know, Alex," I responded and stood there with him, just staring at this beautiful creature God created. I can honestly say that for the next few moments, I realized that in almost fifty years, I truly have never stopped to really, thoroughly enjoy what I was looking at. I stood there with Alex as he stared, not knowing what was going through his mind at the time, but knowing what was going through mine. I was truly experiencing a magnificent animal with beautiful markings and colors and taking it all in, grateful that I could really enjoy what I was seeing and appreciate it. My son does this all the time. He truly enjoys the moment.

He doesn't take things for granted, but appreciates them for what they are and treasures their beauty, magnificence, and awe.

And, he doesn't even realize he does this. He just does it! I realize it and still I don't do it as often as I should. Why not?

We went on to see more animals, and Alex did the same thing with the beautiful peacock as it spread its wings so we could adore the beautiful feathers. The giraffes extended their long necks for us to observe the interesting colors and markings. I don't think I ever really experienced the zoo as I had on that day. And it was because

my son shared something with me that could never be learned any other way than how he taught me.

It reminded me of a saying Father John always uses. He says that one of his favorite bishops says, "If you want to teach others about faith, you only *sometimes* have to use words."

How true that is for me with Alex. He didn't have to stand there at that zoo exhibit taking in the beauty of the animals and tell me, "Mommy, look at them, truly look at them and enjoy them and take in all of their beauty and magnificence and thank God for creating them." He didn't have to tell me that, nor could he in his simple, cognitively impaired speech. But the point is that he didn't have to. I learned it from him by just observing him. He didn't use words; he didn't have to. His actions alone spoke volumes.

24

Seize Every Opportunity

Epilepsy is one of the most common disorders of the nervous system. Autism is a poorly understood mental disorder that can severely impair a child's ability to comprehend and communicate. Down Syndrome is a human disorder caused by the production of a cell with an extra chromosome. Each of these conditions can include moderate to severe mental deficiency in the individual diagnosed. Each also affects the families of people of all ages, races, and ethnic backgrounds.

Epilepsy, autism, and Down Syndrome are what you have, not what you are. It is a part of your life, but not your whole life. By no means am I trying to downplay the significance of these conditions, because they will most likely affect your life and the lives of those around you profoundly.

> **Attitude and acceptance of this diagnosis will help determine and embrace the best possible outcome.**

Yes, you were given a diagnosis you'd never wish on anybody, but the fact is that you were given it, so embrace it and do something about it. Above all else, learn from it and teach others what you've learned along the way. It's not the end of the world, but the beginning of what could truly turn into a wonderful experience if you let it.

I was talking recently to a father of a young child with Down Syndrome. I was praising his son and telling his father what a joy he has been to me. The father thanked me for the kind words about his son and then said to me, "I wish everyone could have a son like him."

I knew exactly how this father felt. He did not know that I had a special needs son of my own, and yet he felt very confident and sincere to share his sentiments with me. I often feel the same way.

> **I wish everyone could have a son like mine.**

As I go through the journey of raising him, I often ponder two questions: "Why is he here?" and "Where did he come from?" I've been thinking an awful lot about those two questions in particular, and although I might not have the perfect answers to them, I'd like to share with you what I do know.

Why is he here?

I'm a firm believer in the saying, *everything happens for a reason.* I also have a strong sense of faith. I believe in God and I believe in divine intervention. Did God place Alex in my family's life and say, "Here you go. You will have heartache and trials and tribulations with this child, sometimes beyond your comprehension. But with my help, you will get through it and he will bring you love and peace and compassion and joy that you could have never known if you didn't know him"?

I don't know the exact answer to that, but I do know that it is exactly what happened.

A friend of mine is on a peace mission. She's a truly remarkable, inspiring woman and is trying to reach out to the masses, to spread peace and help people live a simpler, more peaceful, and calmer life. She has read numerous books on these topics to learn how to live such a life herself, and to teach others in the process. My son has never read a book in his life; he can't read. Yet, he lives the life she is dreaming about for herself and others.

How? I often wonder. How does he already know the peaceful

existence, live it, and embrace it?

He is definitely in this world for a reason. And maybe that reason is something so simple as to teach us and show us all how to live by his actions. When my husband and I are going some days at full speed and get agitated and short with each other, Alex can sense it. He will tell us to "calm down!" Sometimes I think he doesn't know what's going on around him, and then I realize he knows it better than I.

Nick and I invited friends to join us for dinner so we could catch up. It was going to be a double date, like we used to go on many years ago. We couldn't find a babysitter for Alex, so I called my friend to cancel. As we talked, she said it was just as well because she and her husband were fighting and she didn't feel like going out with him. They had been having some marital problems and had been in counseling for quite some time. As we talked, Nick entered the room and said, "Let's just take Alex with us."

I agreed. After all, he needed to eat too, he enjoys restaurants, and he really likes the couple we were going out with. After some coaxing, my friend agreed that they would join us.

It turned out to be a "better than expected" evening, with Alex in tow. The next morning, my friend called me to talk. She's not the most positive person in the world, and she caught me a bit off guard when she thanked me for encouraging her to go out. She said her and her husband would have probably just stayed home and fought, and that Alex always makes her feel better.

She mentioned that as soon as they entered the restaurant, Alex hugged her and told her that she was beautiful. As time goes on, and we take each other and our relationships for granted, it's not often enough that we hear things like that. Alex was honest and sincere. He meant every word he said to her, and she knew it and felt it coming from him. She continued by telling me that she and her husband actually had a pleasant evening after they left us and she said it was because

Alex showed her what's important after all.

Did Alex actually tell her that? No! He couldn't even come up with the words. They are not in his simple vocabulary. But he showed her that night at the restaurant by his actions, gestures, kind words, and smile.

Where did he come from?

God blessed me with Alex nineteen years ago as I brought him into the world. Whenever anyone asks Alex, "How are you?" his usual response is, "I'm happy." And they usually smile. I wanted more from him one day so I asked him, "Alex, why are you happy?"

He responded, "Because I am!"

I probed a little further, wanting to know more, wanting my son to teach me more. So I said, "Is it because you're special?"

He looked at me and simply said, "Mommy, I'm happy because I'm special." I thought to myself, there's my answer!

But then Alex continued, "I'm special, and you're special, and Daddy's special, and Kellie's special, and Angela's special, and Nicholas is special."

Wow, I thought to myself. He not only thinks he's special, but he thinks each one of us is special, and he's absolutely right—we all are. In God's eyes, we are all special, each and every one of us, and my son knows that. And he's always happy just because he exists. Why isn't each and every one of us? My nineteen-year-old special needs son with an IQ of an eight-year-old, who has never read a single book in his life, including the Bible, already knows more than I do about the importance of life. How can that be?

Our family attended a baccalaureate mass at our local parish. Father John gave a great homily to all of the recent graduates, including Alex. He told them that God has a plan for everyone. The only way to be truly happy is to follow the plan that God has in store for you. Too often, people try to fight the plan laid out for them and therefore have a hard time finding true happiness. Maybe that's why Alex is simply "happy" all the time. He has accepted the path God has in store for him and embraced it. He must understand this better than the rest of us, because he truly is the happiest of anyone I know.

Alex is definitely here for a reason and he'll leave a legacy that I can only dream of. He already has. I can't wait to see what the future holds for him and the rest of the world, for nothing is beyond his reach. He's already proven that. He has taught me more about life and humility than I could have ever taught him—simply because he is here!

25

Graduation

"Mommy, why are you crying? You should like my pictures. You should be happy!"

Alex, seated in the passenger seat next to me, looked concerned. I looked at him and began crying some more. Through the tears, I turned to him and said, "Honey, I *am* happy and your pictures look great...these are happy tears."

Confused, he responded, "You can't be happy when you cry."

Just moments earlier, Alex and I had walked into the portrait studio to pick up his senior picture proofs. There was a middle-aged woman standing at the counter looking at her son's senior pictures. You could tell by the smile on her face, her demeanor, and the quality of the pictures that she was indeed very proud of her son. He was a handsome boy, to be sure, and I noticed the pictures she had of him in his varsity football uniform. She referred to her son as "a good-looking, talented athlete."

I glanced at the pictures and thought, *Gee, I hope Alex's pictures turned out as nice.*

Just then, the photographer handed me Alex's pictures and I was immediately filled with pride. Even though Alex could never play a contact sport like football, or earn a varsity letter, or receive a driver's license, he was a senior in high school and preparing to graduate. I personally never thought I would be able to enjoy this graduation milestone with our third child. I didn't realize how much it would matter to him, as well as me. Every day with him is truly a gift, and I'm grateful that I get to treasure what he brings into my life.

Alex in his cap and gown.

On Saturday, June 6, 2009, my son graduated from his high school with the rest of the class of 2009. Just like his peers, he walked proudly across that stage in a blue cap and gown, proud of the past twelve years and all that he had accomplished. Unlike most of the seniors in his graduating class, he did not receive a high school diploma or receive high honors for his grades. He wasn't recognized as a member of the National Honor Society. Nor did he anticipate entering college in the fall as the next phase of his life. Yet, Nick and I were so proud of him and very grateful too.

Proud, because even though he did not receive a diploma, he did receive a certificate of completion for high school. Proud, because of all he has accomplished over the past eighteen years of his life. Proud, because of what he has taught us and what he has become.

Grateful, for those with special needs children that came before us and had a vision to give special needs children the same high school experience that is awarded to every other child of high school age. Grateful that, because of them, our son was able to experience high school with his peers and rites of passage such as dances, homecomings, prom, football games, field trips, and graduation parties.

Alex's graduating class.

The day after the ceremony, we hosted a graduation party to celebrate this milestone with Alex. Like everything else about Alex, this party wasn't all about him. Sure, he was proud to graduate just like his two older siblings, and he wanted to wear his cap and gown for the second day in a row and serve sloppy joes to his guests.

But unlike my other children, his list of party guests was quite different.

He invited the physical therapist, who makes him work "so hard" and exercise so his muscles won't remain too tight. He always has a smile for her and charms her with his kind words. "You're beautiful," he tells her, because she is—inside and out—to him.

He invited all the priests from our local parish who sometimes "make church too long," but only because he can't wait to see them after mass, shake their hands, and request I take a picture of him with them.

He invited the many babysitters he's had over the years. He enjoys spending time with them, even though he tells us "babysitters are for babies." We tell him they are just coming over to hang out with him for a little while.

He invited the bus driver and bus aide who make sure he gets to school safely and on time, even though he says six-thirty is too early and too dark outside to go to school.

He invited the nice cashier from the grocery store who always takes the time to talk to him and ask him about his day. He tells her she's "beautiful" too.

He invited his teachers who have made, I'm guessing, as much difference in his life as he has made in theirs. That's just the type of child he is—sincere, giving, and always the charmer!

Just before the guests were to arrive, I told Alex to welcome each guest by looking them in the eye, shaking their hand, and saying, "Thank you for coming to my party."

He listened to me intently as I spoke. I thought he would practice by repeating at least a portion of what I said to him. Instead he looked at me and said, "I can't say all that!"

I had to laugh for I knew I was throwing way too much at him to catch. I would just have to leave it up to him and fate, and I honestly knew, deep down, that everything would work out.

Unlike Nicholas's and Kellie's parties, I didn't worry about rain or people not showing up. One of Alex's teachers told me, "It's Alex. Of course the day will turn out just fine." She meant that and I knew that would be the case. And it was!

As the guests arrived, Alex would run up to greet them with a big smile, and I would take a picture of him with each family that arrived. He enjoyed this very much. I love taking "memories," and Alex loves looking through all the photo books I put together and reminiscing about what happened when the pictures were taken. As I was busy talking with some friends, Alex came quickly to my side and shouted to me, "Mommy, Mommy, the beautiful girls are here!"

I excused myself and let Alex drag me to the driveway. I anticipated meeting some of the mainstream education senior girls that assisted in his classroom. Instead, I was greeted by Katelyn and Alissa and their families. Both girls have Down Syndrome and participated in his special education program. I was not surprised to see them since Alex had invited them. But I was surprised because I was not expecting to see them at that particular moment. I was expecting to see the girls who helped in his classroom.

Alex and the "beautiful girls" at his graduation party.

These two girls are very dear to Alex. When he referred to them as the "beautiful girls," it was with the most sincere, honest, genuine heart that you could ever imagine. As I've said before, my son can read people quite well. To Alex, these two sweet, adorable eighteen-year-old girls were indeed "beautiful," for he truly sees people for who they are—obviously, better than I do!

The next weekend, Alex and I attended Alissa's graduation. As we walked into her backyard, he noticed Katelyn was already there and was talking to Alissa. He said to me, "Look, Mommy, the beautiful girls are here."

"I know; I see them," I responded back to him.

Alissa's mom heard this and after thanking us for coming, she said, "You know, when we attended Alex's party, I heard him refer to Alissa as a beautiful girl and my heart just melted." A tear ran down her cheek as she spoke.

> "People tell me all the time that she's special, or a blessing, but no one has ever told me, or her, that she's beautiful."

I listened as she continued to speak. "Joan, when you walked in, I heard Alex call her 'beautiful' again, and I have to tell you my heart leaped with joy. Your son is so sweet to say that and I truly know how much he means it. You don't know how much that means to me." At that point she hugged me and tears flowed down her cheeks. I was deeply touched and knew how much my son's honest, sincere words meant to this mother of a Down Syndrome child. I've walked in her shoes and know people can be so cruel as they stare and poke fun at our special needs children. Alex's comments meant the world to her.

Her husband was standing next to her, taking all of this in, and he reached for my hand, shook it, pulled me in, and gave me a hug also.

"Thank you," he said, and I could see his eyes well up.

As I glanced over at my son, towering over his "beautiful" friends, I was the proudest mother on the face of the earth. Alex has taught me in ways I never dreamed possible.

> He says what he means and means what he says better than anyone I have ever known.

A few days after the party, I was having a conversation with my oldest brother, whose advice I greatly appreciate and respect. He was unable to attend Alex's party because he was working out of the country at the time. I was telling him what a successful day it was, and he asked me to define success.

I was caught off guard. I didn't answer right away, but told him I would get back to him. I wanted to think about it. We continued the conversation a few days later and I said to him, "The dictionary defines success as 'a favorable or satisfactory outcome or result,' but society defines it loosely as the gaining of wealth and fame."

He then responded, "Well, according to the dictionary, your son is a success!" Tears rolled down my face and joy filled my heart!

26
An Idyllic Life

We all long for the ideal life, but so far none of us has been able to achieve it. We want that standard of perfection in our marriages and our jobs and from our kids and even on our vacations. But often we find that the ideal we are looking for only exists in our imaginations.

I recently planned a summer vacation for my family. The six of us were going to spend a week at the beach in Florida. We would enjoy all that Florida has to offer, as well as each other's company. It would be the perfect getaway, the ideal family vacation. In my mind, I had the whole week planned out. Nick and I were going to enjoy fun in the sun, dinners on the waterfront, and lovely sunsets with our four children. I had the perfect scenario mapped out in my mind. I hadn't planned for any doom and gloom in this picture at all. After all, we worked hard and deserved a perfect vacation without any glitches, right?

Wrong! Now let's get back to reality. This is life, after all, and life isn't always perfect or ideal. In fact, it is often filled with the good, the bad, and the ugly. And often all three can come into play when we least expect it. When the reality of life sets in, like it always does, we need to decide how we are going to react to it.

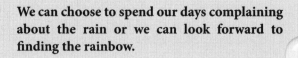

We can choose to spend our days complaining about the rain or we can look forward to finding the rainbow.

As our trip to Florida drew near, Nick was having many problems at work. We realized that he could not come with us. He did join us for the last three days but he spent most of that time on his laptop and cell phone with work-related problems back home. We gave him his space.

My oldest son developed a stomach virus in Florida and ended up spending two days in bed and near a bathroom. We gave him his space for some much needed rest.

The second day of our trip, Alex had a seizure. We couldn't go out to dinner as a family that night. We had to let him sleep it off.

It was ninety-nine degrees and very hot and humid.

Now, let's look at the positive...

My husband put the laptop and cell phone away for one full day and totally engaged in the family activities we had planned. The six of us walked the beach, collected seashells, swam in the Gulf of Mexico, drank margaritas, and enjoyed a delicious dinner at a lovely waterfront restaurant. It was wonderful! Nick got to spend one full day with us, which was far better than none.

My eldest son perked up after some much needed rest and plenty of fluids. He joined in the fun for the rest of the week. He actually took on the role of his missing father and was rather good at it. Alex kept telling him, "Nicholas, you are the daddy when he's not here." It was cute.

Alex rested after his seizure for the rest of that evening and I got to finish reading a book I never had time for. I truly enjoyed my book and the peace and quiet around me for an entire evening. I sent my other three children out to explore the beach town and they had a good time doing so. They brought back carry-out food for Alex and me. They were reluctant to go after Alex's incident, which I found very touching, but I encouraged them to go. I am always trying to figure out how to have the best possible life for me and my family within the parameters of caring for my son.

The warm, hot, sunny weather allowed us to swim and sun ourselves to our heart's content, and that was quite enjoyable, especially with the backdrop of gorgeous palm trees everywhere. It was indeed postcard perfect and I was grateful.

The Broggis enjoying their idyllic Florida vacation.

Dwelling on the negative, our trip wasn't ideal by any means. In fact, it was full of obstacles.

But

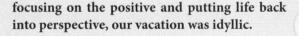

focusing on the positive and putting life back into perspective, our vacation was idyllic.

One of my favorite living artists is Thomas Kinkade. He truly uses his gifts to inspire others. I enjoy not only his paintings, but his words of wisdom too. I have his 2009 calendar entitled "The Art of Choosing a Joyful Life." It is full of beautiful paintings and inspirational messages. One of my favorite quotes is, "When we keep ourselves tuned to the beauty of the world, life itself becomes a joyous celebration of the senses."

When I think of a Thomas Kinkade painting, I think of an idyllic setting—a scene of simplicity and happiness with a touch of love thrown in. That to me sums up his paintings.

The other day after dinner, I made Alex one of his favorite desserts. Before he took a bite of the strawberry shortcake I placed in front of him, he looked at it with the biggest blue eyes. He then smelled it and said, "Mmm, this smells so good." Then he took a bite and stated, "Mmm, this tastes so good." Obviously he was enjoying his dessert immensely.

"Thank you, Mommy" he then told me.

"For what?" I asked him.

"For making me my favorite dessert."

"You're welcome," I responded.

He was indeed truly grateful and was savoring every bite of this dessert. *How often do we do that?* I had to wonder to myself. I often eat my food so fast I don't even really taste it. And I surely don't take the time to really look at it, or smell it, or be truly grateful for it like he does. *Why not?* I had to wonder again.

When I think of Alex, I am reminded of the simplicity and happiness and joy he brings into my world. That to me sums up my son.

I may not live the ideal life, but my son has taught me how to live an idyllic life!

Alex and his sister Kellie.

As I reflect back on the last nineteen years and all that has happened to Alex and our family during the course of his illness, there are several things I have learned that I would like to share with parents of special needs children.

Be an advocate. You are your child's best advocate, and nobody in this entire universe will look out for him or her more than you can and will.

- Get involved. Learn all you can about the available programs. Push for services, such as speech, physical, and occupational therapy.

- Discipline them. Do not be afraid to give them consequences when they misbehave, for they need that, just like any other child.

- Educate your child to the best of their ability, and educate others as well. Education is of key importance. People that make fun of our kids are not necessarily mean; they are just uneducated. They do not know any better, because they are not familiar with our children's needs and conditions. Not everyone understands a special needs child. We can change that by educating them.

- Love them unconditionally. Granted you will encounter struggles and difficulties along the way, but you will also experience the unspeakable joy they will bring into your lives.

Whether you have a special needs child or not, understand that our lives are shaped by our families and the people that surround us. My son has taught me that it doesn't really matter how much you possess or own, it's what's in your heart that matters. Be selfless and give of your time and talents to reach out to others. People are much more important and have far greater value than things. Everyone faces adversity and setbacks in life. It's what you do with those times and how you react to them that form your character. Learn from them and teach others. Focus on what's good in every situation. If you look hard enough, there is always good, even when life seems bleak. Do not place emphasis on what you *want* but rather on what you *need*. Be grateful every day for the blessings God has given you; they far outweigh the obstacles. We learn better from the hardships than from the goodness in our lives. Take those opportunities to prioritize your life and recognize what truly matters. It is the people and relationships in our lives—not the things—that will bring us lasting joy.

Alex will probably never mentally reach an age past eight or ten years old, and I've come to terms with that. I can't undo the brain damage and although I've often wished he'd grow out of the seizures and become "normal," I know it may never happen. I've come to embrace the things he is and has become, rather than what he's not or never will be. He has a great innocence about him that is so very inspiring. Although I know he will not grow up to make a lot of money—he will grow up to make a difference. He already has!

I'm not sure what the future holds for him, but we'll take that journey together and learn from each other along the way as we've always done. One of my friends has a special needs child also, and she once told me that she didn't know what would happen to her child after she and her husband passed away. "I don't want to burden the siblings," she told me.

I used to think the same. The more I thought about it though, I realized I wouldn't be burdening Alex's siblings with him. There's a joke in our family that Angela gets to take care of me in my old age, and I'll probably drive her crazy with all of my jokes and silly talk. Nicholas, our eldest son, gets to take care of his dad, and they'll probably drive each other crazy because they are more alike than either cares to admit. Kellie will take care of Alex (Brother Bear, as she calls him), because of their close bond and the fact that she will be an experienced occupational therapist. All the kids agree on this arrangement, saying that Kellie is the lucky one!

It should never be considered a "burden" to care for loved ones. I know that this is what family does for each other. They take care of each other and never give up on one another.

A burden—no. A reality—yes, and one we need to deal with and embrace the best we know how.

This journey I've walked with my son was one I never would have expected. Yet, it turned out to be one of the best experiences of my life. And I will continue the journey as long as I am physically able.

When people tell you they are blessed with a special needs child, take it from someone who knows—we are blessed, and we truly mean what we say. I've been through a lot with Alex—ups and downs, good and bad, difficulties and triumphs—and I wouldn't trade any of it for anything else in this entire world. He taught me the difference between wants and needs. I was the one that needed to be cured, not him. He is perfectly fine just the way he is.

I got exactly what I needed. I didn't realize it at the time. In fact, I often fought against it—wishing, hoping, and praying for something else. But, sometimes, those things in life that we think are problems actually turn out to be solutions. Like the lyrics to one of my favorite Rolling Stones songs that refers to not getting what you want but getting what you need, I got what I needed!

Because of a special gift from God I received in a hospital delivery room over nineteen years ago, I have become better.

A better person.

A better wife.

A better mother.

A better Christian.

A better example.

My life has not only been changed by this child, but also enriched beyond measure. I am excited to see how much more he can teach me!

The Essence of Alex

The Beatitudes are the nine declarations of blessedness made by Jesus in the Sermon on the Mount. They are described in Matthew 5:1–12 (New American Bible). They are ideals which we should pursue constantly in our lives if we are to live justly and humbly. It is not easy to do. Alex has exemplified these concepts.

Blessed are the poor in spirit, for theirs is the kingdom of heaven.

Alex does not own a home, a car, or material possessions. These things are not important to him at all. His confidence is in God.

Blessed are they who mourn, for they will be comforted.

Alex has suffered mental and physical anguish throughout his entire life. His belief in God has never wavered.

 Blessed are the meek, for they will inherit the land.

Alex has taught his family the true meaning of humility. He has such a gentle spirit and is most patient and kind.

 Blessed are they who hunger and thirst for righteousness, for they will be satisfied.

Alex knows right from wrong, and he holds himself and others accountable to meeting the standards of what is morally right.

 Blessed are the merciful, for they will be shown mercy.

Alex always treats others, no matter their status, with the utmost kindness and compassion. He sees everyone as equals.

 Blessed are the clean of heart, for they shall see God.

Alex is always sincere and has one of the purest hearts of anyone I have ever known.

Blessed are the peacemakers, for they will be called children of God.

Alex leads a calm and serene life and through his actions, encourages others to do likewise.

Blessed are they who are persecuted for the sake of righteousness, for theirs is the kingdom of heaven.

Alex is not always treated with the utmost respect that every human being is deserving of, yet he remains unassuming and scrupulous.

Blessed are you when they insult you and persecute you and utter every kind of evil against you (falsely) because of me. Rejoice and be glad, for your reward will be great in heaven.

Alex is not affected by mean words or the stares directed at him due to his disability. Instead, he is strong in character, faith, and spirit because of it.

Acknowledgments

I would like to personally thank the following individuals for helping to make this book a reality:

- My publisher, Marian Nelson, for embracing this project and believing in me.

- My project manager, Erin Braun, for her kindness and professionalism.

- My husband, Nick, for supporting this endeavor every step of the way.

- My daughters, Kellie and Angela, for all their help, input, and typing assistance.

- My pastor, Fr. John Riccardo, for increasing and strengthening my awareness of the faith through his gift of teaching.

- Christina McAuliffe and Heather O'Connor, for always being available to care for Alex whenever called upon.

- Ellen Stefaniak and Mary Jarvis, for encouraging me to tell this story to help others "in the same shoes."

- My nephew, Joseph McAuliffe, for making the DVD.

- My professional photographer, Tammy, for all her help and generosity.

A portion of the proceeds will benefit the following charities:

The Epilepsy Foundation of Michigan
20300 Civic Center Dr. Ste. 250
Southfield, MI
48076
www.epilepsymichigan.org

Special Olympics Michigan
Central Michigan University
Mt. Pleasant, MI
48859
www.somi.org

Joan Broggi is a substitute special education teacher. She has been teaching children, including those with special needs, for the past eight years.

The impact Alex has had on other people's lives has been remarkable. Joan realized the breadth of Alex's impact when she experienced the love and joy bestowed upon Alex at his high school graduation. This outpouring of affection led Joan to put pen to paper and write *Bursting with Joy*. She hopes this story inspires others.

Joan graduated from the University of Michigan and is one of eight children. In her free time, she enjoys most sporting events, spending time with her family, and taking pictures to capture all of life's special moments.

Joan resides in southeastern Michigan with her husband, Nick, their four children, Kellie, Nicholas, Alex, and Angela, and their dog, Jerzi.

You can read more about Alex, Joan, and the entire Broggi family at JoanBroggiBooks.com.

Praise for
Bursting with Joy

Bursting with Joy is one of the most heart-warming, sensitive stories told by a mother through her son's eyes. Joan Broggi captures true lessons of life that every parent or reader could learn from. She delicately expresses her son's innocent, yet very honest way of looking at the world. The book is a necessary read for anyone who is a parent, young or old, and especially for parents who have children with disabilities.

Ellen Stefaniak,
Special Education Consultant

Bursting with Joy is an engaging, intimate, and very real look into the everyday challenges, graces, and gifts that are part of raising a son or daughter with special needs. Perhaps especially for a culture that so often defines greatness by what someone *does*, Joan reminds us all that real greatness is defined by who one *is*.

Rev. John Riccardo,
Pastor at Our Lady of Good Counsel Catholic Church